Richmond Today
Including Kew Gardens and Hampton Court

Richmond upon Thames is the most beautiful borough in London. Famous for Hampton Court and Kew Gardens, it contains more historic delights than any other, except Westminster and the City's square mile.

In this new portrait Roger George Clark looks at 850 years of Richmond's history. Here came the medieval kings, the Tudors – including Henry VIII and Elizabeth I – and later the Stuarts and Hanoverians. George II and George III had summer residences in Richmond and Kew; Queen Victoria stayed in White Lodge. The borough also has connections with four princes who became twentieth-century monarchs – Edward VII, George V, Edward VIII and George VI – and associations with three queens – Alexandra, Mary and Queen Elizabeth the Queen Mother. Three royal parks lie within its boundaries

Richmond has attracted visitors as diverse as Samuel Pepys, Horatio Nelson, the last Tsar Nicholas II and Charlie Chaplin. General Eisenhower organized the 1944 Allied invasion of Europe in Bushy Park. Writers and artists abound – Francis Bacon, Alexander Pope, Horace Walpole (whose Strawberry Hill villa inspired the first horror story), Henry Fielding, Charles Dickens, Alfred, Lord Tennyson, George Eliot, Henry James and Virginia Woolf. Noel Coward started life here in genteel poverty. Sir Joshua Reynolds, Turner, Van Gogh, Pissarro and Sisley knew the district well. The composer Gustav Holst lived in a house overlooking the river. The Beatles made *A Hard Day's Night* and *Help!* in a local studio while Mick Jagger, Tommy Steele, Sir John Mills, the Attenboroughs, the Dimblebys and numerous other celebrities made it their home.

International fame came to Twickenham with rugby and to Mortlake with the Oxford and Cambridge Boat Race.

The author explores in words and pictures riverside villas, secret islands and historic boatyards which marshalled the Little Ships that set sail for Dunkirk. He visits the villages and churches that give Richmond upon Thames its unique character. And he discovers the secret of the Hampton Court Maze.

Roger George Clark has lived in Richmond upon Thames since he was at school. He knows the district intimately and as a student rowed up and down the Boat Race course more frequently than many varsity men. He has taken photographs for more than twenty years; his pictures are in the National Portrait Gallery and have been exhibited at the Royal National Theatre. His previous books include *The Isle of Wight, Henley the Regatta* (with Daniel Topolski) and *Chelsea Today*. Roger George Clark has reported London affairs for many years on BBC Radio and broadcasts on the World Service and Radio 4. Previously he worked on the *Observer* and in publishing.

D1335952

Richmond Today

Including Kew Gardens and Hampton Court

ROGER GEORGE CLARK

ROBERT HALE · LONDON

ISBN 0 7090 5115 8

Robert Hale Limited
Clerkenwell House
Clerkenwell Green
London EC1R 0HT

2 4 6 8 10 9 7 5 3 1

Photoset in North Wales by
Derek Doyle & Associates, Mold, Clwyd.
Printed and bound in Hong Kong by
Bookbuilders Ltd.

Contents

St Mary's parish church, the oldest building in Twickenham and burial place of Alexander Pope. The nave collapsed in 1713 and was rebuilt – a Georgian box adjoining a medieval tower

*May fair on Richmond Green – the scene since medieval times of
pageants, spectacles, sports and jousting by knights in armour. Sheep
once grazed here and there was bull- and bear-baiting*

River God at the entrance to Ham House. Beautifully situated by the Thames and surrounded by parkland, this mansion, where the Cabal met, has survived unaltered from the seventeenth century

A ten-acre lake provides safe waters for sailing, canoeing, windsurfing and powerboating at Thames Young Mariners' Outdoor Education Centre, Ham Fields

Acknowledgements

I would like to thank the staff in the local history departments at Richmond and Twickenham Libraries whose help and enthusiasm made this book possible. The President of the Museum of Richmond, John Cloake, gave invaluable advice. Ann Kaye and Mona Brinton carefully scrutinized the manuscript and their eagle-eyed comments were appreciated.

I would also like to thank Pamela Clark of the Royal Archives. Extracts from Queen Victoria's diary are quoted by gracious permission of Her Majesty The Queen. Susanne Groom at Historic Royal Palaces read the chapter on Hampton Court, Laura Ponsonby at Kew reviewed the chapter on the Royal Botanic Gardens and Norma Stanway of Richmond upon Thames Council looked at the manuscript.

Viscount Sidmouth was kind enough to confirm details about Nelson's visit to White Lodge, while the Dwight D. Eisenhower Library, Abilene, Kansas, provided information about General Eisenhower's activities in Richmond and Bushy Parks.

In addition I would like to thank the following for permission to photograph their premises: the American International University in London (Richmond College), Historic Royal Palaces at Hampton Court; the King's Observatory, Kew; St Mary's College, Strawberry Hill; the Royal Ballet School, White Lodge; St Catherine's Convent (Pope's Grotto); St Paul's School; the Royal British Legion Poppy Factory; the Royal Military School of Music, Kneller Hall; the vicars of St Philip and All Saints, North Sheen, and St Peter's Church, Petersham; Toughs of Teddington; George Sims Racing Boats, Eel Pie Island; J.T. Stephenson at Latchmere House, Ham Common; David Gilmour the owner of Fred Karno's houseboat the *Astoria*.

Richard Lester and Kim Wilkie gave me new perspectives on Richmond, Nicholas Reed helped with information about Kew and scores of people too numerous to mention gave assistance. Any errors are mine.

Barnes, a thriving town, retains its country atmosphere near the former school overlooking the pond, once the centre of village life

1   This Other Eden?

One spring day in 1965, a quiet suburban street, renowned only for an occasional clink of a milk bottle or knock on the door by a postman, was thrown into turmoil. Four young men jumped out of a Rolls-Royce, pushed open four garden gates, dashed up the pathways, slid keys into the locks and entered four drab-looking terraced houses set side by side. The front doors opened into a vast air-conditioned room crammed with millionaires' gadgets – sunken beds, a Mighty Wurlitzer rising from the cellar, vending machines spewing sandwiches and drinks, revolving bookshelves and electronic marvels. There was also grass on the floor.

The young men were the Beatles, who were shooting the opening scenes of their second film *Help!* It was the height of Beatlemania. International frenzy had engulfed the Fab Four. Screaming fans surged up and down the street while police tried to control the crowds.

The extraordinary interior existed only in a film studio, but the terraced houses were real. Numbers 5, 7, 9 and 11 Ailsa Avenue, St Margarets, soon became known worldwide as the Beatles' London home. And the location was a short distance from Twickenham Film Studios in Richmond upon Thames where *Help!* and its predecessor, *A Hard Day's Night*, were made.

The Beatles' acquaintance with the district was fleeting, but the film's director, Richard Lester, made it his home. 'Richmond always had that quality of being the troublesome place,' he said. 'It was slightly out of the ordinary and slightly weird, right from the time it was called Shene in the thirteenth and fourteenth centuries when barges came sweeping along the river for a rave-up! All the houses built to service the two major palaces were for the upper classes hanging-on-crowd. The Rolling Stones first played here. There was a very early drug scene here – much earlier than any of the other boroughs.'

Indeed the Stones' lead singer, Mick Jagger, occupied one of the grandest houses on Richmond Hill, overlooking the famous view painted by Turner and Reynolds and admired by Mendelssohn. Down below in Petersham the singer and entertainer Tommy Steele settled in an eighteenth-century mansion, while across the river in Twickenham Pete

*A heron takes flight near Richmond Bridge. The
river provides a green corridor through one of
the richest wildlife areas in London*

Townsend of The Who took up residence in the former home of the Victorian Poet Laureate Alfred, Lord Tennyson.

'Funny, louche, subtle,' was how the architectural critic Ian Nairn described Richmond in the 1960s. 'A bit of Wimbledon, a bit of Windsor and a disturbing whiff of Soho or Brighton.' From earliest times the area had attracted 'much society of note and notoriety', observed a 1973 guide book with a sniff of disapproval. A few years later the local historian John Cloake wrote, 'Three Rs have determined the development of Richmond: Royalty, the River and the Railway.' It was the kings and queens of England who first brought fame and prosperity and gave Richmond its name. As early as Henry I's reign, Shene (as Richmond was originally known) was a separate manor belonging to the Crown. As the royal residence became more important between the fourteenth and seventeenth centuries, a small town grew up. Here came the medieval kings, the Tudors – including Henry VIII and Elizabeth I – and later the Stuarts and Hanoverians. The last British king to lead troops in battle, George II, lived at Richmond Lodge. George III, denounced as 'a tyrant' in the American Declaration of Independence, made Kew the centre of his family life. And his wayward son, the Prince Regent (later George IV), grew up there.

Richmond Park, one of three royal parks that grace the borough, was created by Charles I. After the Restoration the proximity of Windsor, Hampton Court and Kew made Richmond popular with courtiers and officers of state. They left behind grand houses and some of the best Queen Anne and Georgian domestic architecture in Britain. In their wake followed diplomats, politicians, professional men and, in the 1840s after the railway appeared, affluent Victorian commuters.

White Lodge in Richmond Park has been a royal residence on many occasions. Queen Victoria lived here for a few weeks after the death of her mother, the Duchess of Kent. The lodge also welcomed four future twentieth-century monarchs. Edward VII came here as Prince of Wales and brought his consort Alexandra. This secluded building was the childhood home of Queen Mary. She and her husband George V stayed here when their son Edward VIII (who abdicated and became Duke of Windsor) was born. George VI and Queen Elizabeth (the Queen Mother) spent the first years of their marriage at White Lodge. The most surprising guests were the last Tsar and Empress of Russia, Nicholas and Alexandra, who were murdered during the Bolshevik Revolution in 1918.

In addition to royalty, Richmond attracted writers, artists and shadier characters. Francis Bacon owned an estate at Twickenham Park. Samuel Pepys recorded in his diary numerous excursions to the locality, including a visit to Hampton Court in the summer of 1665, followed by nocturnal hanky-panky with Nan, a servant-girl and sailor's wife. Sixty years later Daniel Defoe praised Richmond for its 'noble houses' in *A*

Autumn in Richmond Park. Created by Charles I as a hunting ground, this historic deer chase is the largest royal park in London

Tour Through the Whole Island of Great Britain and noted that here one could find 'a great deal of the best company in England.'

The acerbic Alexander Pope resided in a villa in Twickenham and is buried in the parish church. Horace Walpole's castle at Strawberry Hill inspired the first Gothic novel. Henry Fielding lived in Twickenham and Barnes overlooking the pond on the Green; William Cobbett worked as a gardener at Kew; Charles Dickens wrote a large part of *Nicholas Nickelby* in Petersham and George Eliot first assumed her pen name in Richmond when she began writing novels. Henry James thought Richmond 'the most beautiful' of London's fringes. 'To speak of Richmond Park,' he declared in 1877, 'is to speak of one of the loveliest spots in England.' The author enjoyed boating and strolling along the river banks, while Jerome K. Jerome was inspired by his adventures on the Thames to write the comic novel *Three Men in a Boat*. Virginia Woolf called the Thames 'my river' and Richmond 'the first of the suburbs'. Even Margaret Thatcher fell under Richmond's spell. When she paid a brief visit as Prime Minister in 1983 she stood near the summit of the hill and declared, 'This is the most beautiful view of the Thames I've ever seen.'

Actors came too: David Garrick lived in a stately villa at Hampton (Dr Johnson and James Boswell were guests); Edmund Kean suffered a melancholy end in a theatre on Richmond Green and in the early 1900s Noel Coward grew up in genteel poverty at Teddington. A few years later the music hall impresario Fred Karno moored a fabulous houseboat and floating love-nest at Tagg's Island where he entertained Charlie Chaplin. And the ultimate screen lover of his day, Errol Flynn, began his film career in Teddington Studios.

Sir John Mills, the Attenboroughs, the Dimblebys (who own a local newspaper group), the royal photographer Norman Parkinson and numerous other celebrities have made Richmond upon Thames their home. The Olympic athlete Sebastian Coe lived for a time on the Twickenham waterfront before entering Parliament, while the Russian ballet dancer Rudolf Nureyev, who fled to the West from the Soviet Union, had a house near Richmond Park.

Likewise painters: Turner built a villa in Twickenham and created hundreds of paintings and drawings of the district. In the autumn of 1876 the young Vincent Van Gogh, who had yet to reveal his gifts as an artist, came to Richmond and Petersham to preach in local churches. At the turn of the century the impressionist Pissarro painted on Kew Green and Sisley set up his easel at Hampton Court. Meanwhile, the composer Gustav Holst moved to Richmond and later occupied a house in Barnes overlooking the river.

Besides people of note, this London borough contains more historical sites than any other except Westminster and the City's square mile. Hampton Court Palace, Kew Gardens and Twickenham Rugby Football

Feeding ducks, geese, swans and gulls – a traditional
pastime for parents and children on Twickenham's
waterfront. Eel Pie island lies in the background

Brewer's Lane, one of the oldest streets in Richmond, runs down to the Green. Shops have stood here since Elizabethan times and one house dates back to the 1690s

*Secondhand bookshop, Richmond Hill,
one of many in the borough*

*Noel Coward's childhood home in Walde-
grave Road, Teddington*

*Norman Parkinson poses unabashed in front of the water
nymphs at York House. They were brought to Twickenham
from Italy in 1909*

Ground are world renowned. Each year the Oxford and Cambridge Boat Race brings a day's fame to Mortlake. Other places less celebrated are nonetheless intriguing. In the 1930s that indefatigable writer Arthur Mee, who described 10,000 English towns and villages in his books, stumbled upon 'one of the most extraordinary churches we have come upon in our travels' – a vast Tudor barn transported beam by beam from the countryside and re-erected in North Sheen.

Ham House has the best preserved Jacobean interior in Britain. York House boasts the most daring fountain in London, where naked water nymphs flaunt themselves in front of the local vicarage. Marble Hill was the home of two royal mistresses. At Kew Observatory George III climbed the narrow stairs to gaze at the heavens through a telescope, while Nelson's mistress, Lady Hamilton, lived for a year in misery close to Richmond Bridge.

Less than two miles away in Crane Park are the remains of a gunpowder mill. The ground is torn and undulating where the area was shaken by explosions. And a visitor with a taste for the macabre can go to a churchyard in Mortlake, peer inside the tomb of the Victorian explorer Sir Richard Burton and see his dust-covered coffin.

At Teddington the Victorians built half a cathedral opposite the church where the founder of *The Times*, John Walter, is buried. Along the river bank and amongst the trees on secluded islands lie boatyards that built racing boats, millionaires' yachts and warships for two World Wars. From the Thames the Little Ships set sail in 1940 to rescue the British army trapped in Dunkirk, while in Bushy Park General Dwight D. Eisenhower set up the headquarters where he organized the Allied invasion of Europe in 1944.

Hidden away in Ham is the most sinister building of all – the wartime camp where enemy agents were brought in secret for interrogation and threatened with execution. The camp was situated in woodland and even today, despite encroaching suburbs, nearly half the twenty-two square miles of Richmond upon Thames consists of parkland or open space – 'where the countryside comes to town' boasts the council.

One hundred and sixty thousand people now live in this London borough. It was created in 1965 when the Middlesex borough of Twickenham and the Surrey boroughs of Richmond and Barnes were merged. Stretching from St Paul's School and Hammersmith Bridge in the northeast to Platt's Eyot and Hampton Court Palace in the southwest, it is the only borough to straddle the river. The twenty-one miles of wooded river banks are some of the loveliest in the Thames Valley with a seventeenth and eighteenth-century landscape of parks, villas, palaces, water-meadows and gardens between Hampton and Kew.

Originally, the area consisted of about a dozen towns or villages – Richmond, Barnes, Mortlake and East Sheen, Kew, Ham and Petersham,

The Tudor barn that became a church – St Philip and All Saints – brought to North Sheen from Surrey in 1929

Twickenham and Whitton, Teddington and the Hamptons. Some contain historic churches from medieval times and village greens, where for centuries local people have enjoyed fairs, carnivals and sports (W.G. Grace played cricket on Twickenham Green). Barnes, Kew and Ham still possess their village ponds. Benjamin Disraeli was 'enchanted' with Richmond Green. 'I should like to let my house and live there,' he wrote. 'It is still and sweet, charming alike in summer and winter.'

Disraeli had come to visit the Austrian statesman Prince Metternich, who had fled from the continent after the upheavals in 1848, and was now living in the Trumpeters' House. This elegant Georgian mansion stands midway between the Green and the river, near the Victorian railway bridge linking Richmond and Twickenham. And the story of the borough begins here in the Middle Ages for in this once Arcadian setting England's kings built a glorious palace from where they ruled the country.

*   *   *

Richmond acquired its name from the first of the Tudor kings, Henry VII. Before he slew Richard III at Bosworth Field in 1485 and seized power, the small hamlet by the Thames was known as Shene. Some authorities claim the name derived from an ancient word meaning bright and beautiful, like the Thames on a sunny day. Modern historians argue it comes from an Anglo-Saxon word meaning shelter.

Three hundred years before the Tudors, Shene and Kew were part of the manor of Kingston. But Henry I divided them off and created the separate manor of Shene. At this time all that existed were a simple manor house and a cluster of fishermen's cottages.

Edward III transformed the manor house into a palace with magnificent rooms and kitchens. But when he died here in 1377 he was alone, with only his confessor to administer the last rites and his mistress Alice who pulled the rings from his fingers. One of the yeoman of the King's Chamber was Geoffrey Chaucer, who first established southern English as the literary language of England. By 1389 Chaucer had become Clerk of the King's Works under Richard II and was responsible for the construction and repair of ten royal homes, including Richard's manor at Shene, which he mentions in his poem *The Legend of Good Women*.

Shene was the home of Richard II and his queen, Anne of Bohemia. When she died of plague in 1394 the King was overcome with grief. According to the chronicler John Stow, 'besides cursing the place where she died he did also, for anger, throw down the buildings'. Later they were rebuilt and enlarged by the victor of Agincourt, Henry V, and his son, Henry VI.

But it was the first of the Tudors, Henry VII, who brought splendour to

*Flooding, a perennial problem along the riverside,
particularly at Twickenham opposite Eel Pie
Island, where cars can end up under water*

Richmond and gave the district its name. After he seized the crown from Richard III at Bosworth in 1485, Shene Palace became Henry's favourite residence. Arguably the most intelligent king to sit on the English throne, this subtle and able monarch stabilized the country, quelled fractious nobles with crippling fines and accumulated a vast fortune. Henry VII also built the exquisite Gothic chapel that bears his name and tomb in Westminster Abbey. But, despite his ability, Richmond's founder was suspicious, humourless and menacing.

Disaster struck in 1497. The King and his court were about to celebrate Christmas at Shene when fire swept the palace, burning it to the ground. Rewards of £20 were presented to those who found the King's jewels amongst the ashes. Undaunted, Henry ordered immediate rebuilding on the grandest scale. By 1501 a new palace – a *tour de force* in Gothic, built round courtyards like an Oxford or Cambridge college and covering ten acres – had arisen on the ruins. Henry gave the residence the new name of 'Richmond' to commemorate his earldom of Richmond in Yorkshire, which had been his title before he became King. The name encompassed the hamlet and eventually spread to dozens of places round the globe.

Although parsimonious, Henry lavished money on his palace. A contemporary thought it an 'earthly and second Paradise' and the antiquary John Aubrey claimed it resembled the King's Westminster Abbey chapel. Most of the buildings have vanished or changed, but we can still find traces. Part of the red-brick wall surrounding the residence survives in Old Palace Lane, while the gate-house retains the original iron hinges on which huge wooden doors were hung. Henry's coat of arms are above the archway facing the Green – a royal jousting ground for knights in armour. Here, in 1492, the King held a month-long tournament, but the festivities were marred when a competitor with a faulty helmet was killed. 'He was stricken in the mouth', recorded a contemporary, 'his tongue was borne unto the hinder part of his head, and so he died incontinently.'

Through the archway on the left is the Old Wardrobe, where the soft furnishings of the palace were stored. Arches of an arcade now bricked up are visible.

These buildings look out on Old Palace Yard, formerly the Great Court, at the far end of which is the eighteenth-century Trumpeters' House. Here stood the Middle Gate of the palace, topped by stone figures of two boy trumpeters. Today their images, blurred by time, rest amongst flowers in the garden.

The Middle Gate led to another court, adorned with a fountain ornamented with lions, red dragons and heraldic beasts. On the left lay the Chapel Royal where the choristers' singing was 'more divine than human'; to the right, the richly decorated Great Hall – one hundred feet long and forty feet wide – whose carved timber roof rivalled Hampton Court's in magnificence.

*The gateway to Richmond Palace. The magnificent
Tudor residence built in 1501 covered 10 acres,
rivalled Hampton Court and gave Richmond its name*

Beyond, on what is now the Trumpeters' House lawn, rose the royal apartments. Sumptuously furnished, this three-storey building was crowned by towers, turrets and pinnacles topped with golden weather-vanes embellished with the King's arms. As the wind whistled through the intricate metalwork the air was filled with musical humming.

Richmond was the largest and most dazzling of the royal palaces with a library filled with French books, archery grounds, bowling-alleys, tennis-courts, orchards and a maze of smaller buildings, courts and quadrangles.

When the monarch was in residence the palace was a seat of government. The most influential and ambitious men in the land came to the sovereign's household and from it flowed all privilege and every important political decision. One of the most eminent Renaissance scholars and humanists, Erasmus, visited the palace and Dean Colet, who founded St Paul's School, lived in a nearby monastery.

When Henry VII died in the palace on 21 April 1509 his son, who had spent much of his youth in Richmond, was at his bedside. The next day the new monarch, who was only seventeen, was proclaimed by a herald at the palace gates: 'Henry VIII by the grace of God, King of England and France and Lord of Ireland'. The young King was as flamboyant as his father was austere and soon squandered hoards of gold and jewels as he transformed the court into one of the most opulent in Europe. During the State visit of the Holy Roman Emperor in the summer of 1522, Charles V was entertained at Richmond with pageantry, music, dancing, feasting, hunting, a grand tournament on the Green and masques in the Great Hall. In addition there was serious business. The King and Emperor signed two treaties agreeing to wage war against France.

Henry's first two wives, Catherine of Aragon and Anne Boleyn, knew Richmond Palace well. His fourth wife, Anne of Cleves, retired here after her divorce in 1540 and it was a home for the boy king, Edward VI. Queen Mary – Bloody Mary to her enemies – spent much of her childhood at Richmond and returned on her honeymoon in the summer of 1554 with her husband, Philip II of Spain, who later launched the Armada.

Mary's half-sister Princess Elizabeth, like many of her compatriots, opposed the marriage and was implicated in the rebellion it provoked. After two months' imprisonment in the Tower of London she was brought to Richmond and held under house arrest. Elizabeth, fearing she might be murdered, summoned her Gentleman Usher and asked him and his companions to pray. 'For this night,' she said, 'I think to die.' Her alarm was exaggerated, however, for the Princess was taken to Woodstock and imprisoned.

With Mary's death in 1558 Elizabeth inherited the throne and, despite

*Inside the remains of Richmond Palace – Old
Palace Yard, showing the main Gate, the
Gatehouse and (right) the Wardrobe buildings*

unhappy associations, Richmond became her favourite residence. Thirty years later the palace played a crucial role when England was threatened by the Spanish Armada. From 8 to 29 July 1588 the court sat at Richmond while the Spanish fleet – 130 ships and 30,000 men – sailed up the English Channel. The Privy Council met daily as messages flowed in and out of the palace bringing the latest news and rumours.

By the time the court moved to St James's Palace on 29 July, half the Spaniards' ships were damaged and running for the North Sea and storms finished them off as they limped back home round the Scottish coast. It was too early to establish the extent of victory, but by Christmas Elizabeth and her court were back at Richmond celebrating; the Queen bestowed gold plate on her courtiers and they lavished gold, diamonds, rubies, pearls and garments of the finest silk and velvet upon their Sovereign.

To Richmond came the glittering figures of the age – the Cecils and the Queen's favourites: Robert Dudley, Earl of Leicester (who lived in Kew), and Sir Walter Raleigh. A letter of his exists, written from the palace to the navigator Sir Humphrey Gilbert. The sinister Sir Francis Walsingham lived in a manor house at Barn Elms. He ran an army of spies who uncovered the Armada plans and the plot that enmeshed Mary Queen of Scots in treason and led to her execution.

Men of letters also graced the Richmond court – Sir Philip Sidney, Edmund Spenser and, if one believes some scholars, even Shakespeare. Elizabeth's godson, Sir John Harington, a noted wit, also made a celebrated contribution to civilized living; he built the first flushing lavatory in an English palace.

And it was to Richmond, after a reign of forty-five years, that Elizabeth came to die. In January 1603, although burdened with a heavy cold, the Queen returned to the 'warm winter-box to shelter her old age', as she called the palace.

For weeks the Queen languished in a profound depression, refusing all medical help. She complained of being tired of life, rejected her food, was unable to sleep and rested on the floor. One of her courtiers, Sir Robert Carey, found the Queen in her private quarters 'sitting low upon her cushions' and sighing.

'Madame,' complained the Secretary of State Robert Cecil, 'to content the people you must go to bed.'

'Little man, little man,' replied the Queen, 'the word *must* is not used to princes.'

At three o'clock in the morning of 24 March, Elizabeth passed away in her sleep. A blue ring was presented to Sir Robert Carey by his sister, Lady Scroopes, who had earlier received it from James VI. The King wanted the ring returned when Elizabeth died to prove he had inherited the throne. After some difficulty, Sir Robert left the palace and in sixty

Richmond Green, once an arena for royal tournaments and pageantry, has been the scene of cricket matches since the seventeenth century

Maids of Honour row, built in 1724 on the site of palace buildings overlooking the Green for the women attending Caroline of Anspach

A badly damaged stone trumpeter, which once adorned the Middle Gate of Richmond Palace, now decorates a local garden within the palace precincts

hours galloped with the ring to Edinburgh and informed James he was now King of England as well as Scotland.

His two sons – Henry, Prince of Wales, and Charles – spent part of their childhood at Richmond. But Henry, a radiant prince who embodied many of the nation's hopes, had his life cut short at eighteen. Stricken by illness in 1612, he strove to improve his health by long hours of tennis, hunting and riding. During his last summer he swam in the Thames near the palace 'to the dislike of many', noted his Household Treasurer, Sir Charles Cornwallis, 'who did see him swim after supper, his stomach being full, affirming it to be full of danger, and that it was heedless for him to adventure himself in the water …'

Henry also risked his health in the damp evening air for he delighted 'many times to walk late at night by the river's side in moon light to hear the trumpets sound an echo …'

By November he was dead.

This tragedy had a direct bearing on Richmond Palace, for Henry's less gifted brother, Charles I, became King and roused the country to civil war. He had embellished Richmond with fine paintings and Mortlake tapestries and hunted in the park he created. But after his execution in 1649 the Crown lands were seized and Parliament sold the palace. The Great Hall and Chapel were torn down, the royal apartments destroyed and the stones used for other buildings. Although royalty returned to the neighbourhood, the palace was never rebuilt and only fragments remain to recall its lost splendour.

The continuing royal presence had a profound impact on the landscape between Kew and Hampton where palaces, villas, riverside parks and gardens sprang up. Indeed, the sylvan scene became the cradle of the English Landscape Movement. In a special report on the Thames published in 1994 the landscape architect Kim Wilkie argued this stretch of the river valley had 'become a symbol of idealised English scenery, still inspiring artists, musicians and writers'.

David Coleman of the Countryside Commission was astonished by the sweep of the changes. 'In the seventeenth and eighteenth centuries,' he said, 'courtiers and powerful landowners shaped in a dramatic way the landscape, not just by building their houses and estates, but they developed this gigantic scale of landscape design. It's like a Capability Brown landscape gone mad, with huge-scale vistas and views from one palace to another, deliberately creating picturesque views on a grand scale across an area of one of the largest capital cities in Europe.' This remarkable network of visual connections between buildings and monuments still survives – vistas in Kew Gardens, the meridian in the Old Deer park through the King's Observatory, avenues around Ham House and the setting of Marble Hill – all the way down to the Baroque goose-foot avenues radiating a mile from Hampton Court Palace.

2   Hampton Court

Richmond upon Thames' grandest monument – Hampton Court – was founded by the son of an Ipswich butcher and grazier, Thomas Wolsey. A man of considerable ability and energy, he rose rapidly through the church to become Henry VIII's chief minister. But Wolsey was also vain and greedy, lived in dazzling splendour and kept a lover called Mistress Lark, who bore him two sons.

By 1514 he acquired the lease on a manor-house at Hampton Court, owned by the Knights Hospitallers. To Henry's annoyance Wolsey transformed the dwelling into a palace rivalling Richmond. The Cardinal built a Great Hall where he dined beneath a golden canopy, apartments for the King and Queen, a chapel and long gallery. Out of a thousand rooms 280 were always kept ready to welcome guests. Richly panelled and stuffed with tapestries, rare carpets, precious furniture and silver and gold plate, Hampton Court needed a staff of nearly 500 to manage it. Some idea of the sumptuousness can be gained by visiting Wolsey's Closet – a tiny jewel-box like room, whose intricately decorated ceiling is covered with Tudor roses and Prince of Wales feathers picked out in red, blue and gold. The building also had conveniences rare in Tudor times – lead pipes brought fresh water under the Thames from three miles away, while effluent was carried away from numerous closets by sewers draining into the river.

Hampton Court was only one of Wolsey's residences. His mistake was to outshine the King. By 1525 the Cardinal thought it prudent to present his palace and its entire contents to Henry, the handsomest gift a subject has ever bestowed on a British monarch. Yet it was not enough. Wolsey's failure to secure the Pope's agreement for Henry's divorce from his first wife, Catherine of Aragon, proved his undoing. Four years later Henry confiscated the remainder of his property and arrested him for high treason. The Cardinal died the following year.

Angered by the Pope's intransigence, the King declared himself head of the English Church, destroyed the monasteries and seized their wealth. The money enabled him to engage in extravagant building. He rapidly reconstructed and enlarged Hampton Court, adding a moat,

Hampton Court Palace, Britain's largest Tudor
building, and one of the few that could house the
entire court of 1200 people

drawbridge, courtyards, galleries, new kitchens, three bowling-alleys, a tennis court and tiltyard for tournaments and jousting. Henry himself designed the decorations in his study where he wrote letters and composed accounts. A kiln in the park provided a swift supply of red bricks. Within three and a half years the Great Hall, with a splendid hammerbeam roof, was rebuilt by shifts of masons and carpenters who worked, when necessary, by candlelight. Cellars beneath housed 300 barrels of wine drunk annually by the Tudor court. Wolsey's place of worship became a Chapel Royal of celestial beauty with gilded pendants, angels, cherubs and golden stars twinkling from a ceiling of midnight blue.

In winter the royal court numbered 1,200 people, but only half that in summer when many courtiers went to their own estates. The Great Hall was used for ceremonies and a servants' dining-room. The King ate in his private apartments and senior officials took their meals in the Great Watching Chamber, or Council Chamber. Each year the occupants of Hampton Court consumed 8,200 sheep, 2,330 deer, 1,240 oxen and thousands of calves, pigs, wild boar, larks, swans, peacocks, chickens, sparrows and quails. They also drank 600,000 gallons of ale.

The famous astronomical clock, which is nearly eight feet wide, was made in 1540 by Nicholas Oursian. Set high in Anne Boleyn's gateway, three concentric dials indicate the hour, date, month, number of days since New Year, phases of the moon, signs of the Zodiac and high water at London Bridge – essential information when the Thames was used as a highway between the river palaces, Westminster and the City. The sun is shown revolving round the earth, for the clock was manufactured before the publication of the theories of Copernicus and Galileo.

Henry lived with five of his wives at Hampton Court. Here the future Edward VI was born in October 1537, his birth attended by tragedy for his mother, Jane Seymour, died thirteen days later. And it was here, while Henry was at mass chapel on All Souls' Day 1541, that Archbishop Cranmer handed him a document denouncing his fifth wife for adultery. Aghast, the King initially defended Catherine Howard, but gradually became convinced of her guilt and had her arrested. Legend has it that Catherine slipped her guard and ran to plead her innocence to Henry, who was kneeling at prayer in the chapel. But as she reached the door in the corridor outside, the guards seized her and dragged her away screaming while the King, unmoved, remained on his knees. The gallery is still said to be haunted by her cries. The young Queen, who was barely out of her teens, was beheaded on Tower Green.

For two centuries Hampton Court was a favourite royal residence. Edward VI spent much of his short life here, while his successor, Mary Tudor, received Philip II's proposal of marriage and celebrated part of her honeymoon in the palace. Princess Elizabeth first knew Hampton

The richly decorated and carved hammerbeam roof of Henry VIII's Great Hall, used as a court dining-room and for regal ceremonies

Court as a prisoner, but a year after becoming Queen she returned to live in the palace. Unlike her father and grandfather, Elizabeth I was not a great builder. Nonetheless, visitors were awed by the riches they saw about them. 'All the walls of the palace shine with gold and silver,' wrote the German traveller Paul Hentzner in 1598. He was entranced by a room called Paradise, where 'everything glitters so with silver, gold and jewels as to dazzle one's eyes', while in a corner he noticed a musical instrument 'made all of glass except the strings'. The royal throne was studded with diamonds, rubies and sapphires.

The Duke of Württemberg was amused by a trick fountain and waterworks in Clock Court 'by which you can if you like make the water play upon the ladies and others who are standing by, and give them a thorough wetting'.

Elizabeth enjoyed strolling in the gardens and frequently celebrated Christmas at Hampton Court with hundreds of guests enjoying feasting, hunting, masques, dancing and plays in the Great Hall. And here she was seriously ill with smallpox in 1572, but made a remarkable recovery.

Elizabeth's last recorded visit to the palace was in September 1599 when she was in her sixties. The Queen danced and later departed on horseback in a storm, though she could barely sit upright in the saddle. One of her courtiers, Lord Hunsdon, suggested it was unwise for a person of her years to leave in such weather. 'My years!', exlaimed an enraged Queen. 'Maids, to your horses quickly!' – and she was gone.

Shortly after James I came to the throne he tried to resolve the arguments between the Puritans and the Church of England at the Hampton Court Conference in January 1604. Although the meeting was attended by the Archbishop of Canterbury, sundry bishops, deans and doctors of divinity, as well as the King, the proceedings were far from decorous. A shocked Sir John Harington reported 'the spirit was rather foule mouthed'. The conference did agree, however, to a new translation of the Bible, a decision which a few years later produced a work of incomparable influence and beauty – the Authorised or King James Version of 1611.

Like his predecessors, James I often celebrated Christmas at Hampton Court with masques, dancing and theatre. Inigo Jones designed the scenery and it is almost certain that Shakespeare performed some of his plays, including *Macbeth*, in the Great Hall.

Charles I spent his honeymoon at Hampton Court and embellished the palace with nearly 400 paintings, sculptures, crystal and porcelain. Regrettably, his fabulous collection was sold during the Commonwealth, but Mantegna's nine canvases, the *Triumphs of Caesar*, escaped, and these masterpieces are on show today in their own gallery.

During the Civil War Charles was imprisoned in the palace for eighteen months while Oliver Cromwell tried to negotiate a settlement.

The Great Kitchens – large-scale Tudor catering.
Over fifty rooms covering 36,000 square feet supplied
food for the royal household until Georgian times

Visitors were allowed, including the diarist John Evelyn. 'I came to Hampton Court,' he wrote recalling his meeting on 10 October 1647, 'where I had the honour to kiss his Majesty's hand, he being in the power of these execrable villains who not long after murdered him.'

A month later Charles escaped, leaving behind his pet greyhound whimpering in a corner as he crept out of his room, and slipped quietly down the staircase, through the Paradise Chamber and out into the night. It was raining as the King made his way to the river where horses were waiting. Three days later he arrived in the Isle of Wight, but his plans went awry. He was imprisoned, put on trial and beheaded just over a year after his escape.

Hampton Court survived the worst of Cromwell's excesses only because the Lord Protector himself lived here. When the monarchy was restored, Charles II brought his new bride, Catherine of Braganza, to the palace for their honeymoon. Samuel Pepys saw the royal apartments on 12 May 1662, shortly before her arrival. They were 'nobly furnished', he noted, 'particularly the Queen's bed, given her by the states of Holland. A looking-glass, sent by the Queen Mother from France, hanging in the Queen's chamber. And many brave pictures.'

At the end of the month John Evelyn came to see the bride. She was pretty, he thought, but too short with 'her teeth wronging her mouth by sticking a little too far out'. As for her ladies-in-waiting: 'Never had a pack of such hideous, odious disagreeable women been gathered together to attend a Queen.'

Celebrations took place throughout the summer. From the windows of her bedchamber the new Queen looked out on a spectacular novelty, the Long Water – a monumental canal a mile long, whose banks were lined with a double avenue of 758 lime trees. Excavated the previous winter, it provided a dramatic setting for the festivities where the court could promenade, ride, or float in barges. 'Water had never been used in gardens on this gigantic scale in England before,' observed the art historian Roy Strong. Over 300 years later he thought the Long Water remained 'one of the most staggering and least recognised masterpieces of landscape design in the country … the grandest formal use of water in garden-making in Stuart England.'

Charles II also laid out the rest of the Home Park with radiating avenues of limes and restocked the grounds with game, but Hampton Court was left much as it was. Come the Glorious Revolution of 1688, however, and William of Orange and Mary II decided to pull down the entire palace and build an English Versailles. There was never enough money, though, to compete with the Sun King. When Sir Christopher Wren started work in 1689 he designed a vast new palace, but the final result was bizarre. Henry VIII's State Apartments were destroyed and replaced by a classical building, while two Tudor courtyards remained,

Jean Tijou's exquisite wrought iron-work garden screen

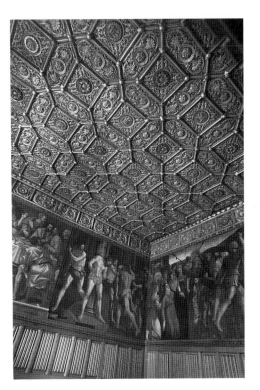

Wolsey's Closet – intricate plasterwork picked out in gold

The great astronomical clock enabled Henry VIII to determine the time, day, month, phases of the moon and high tide at London Bridge

an outcome as curious as any Post-Modernist could wish – a Baroque palace welded on to a Tudor pile, but strangely complementing each other as Wren used orange brick besides Portland stone.

The new building, Fountain Court, resembles a stage set – pleasing to the eye and spectacular from a distance, though closer inspection inside reveals a lack of lavish detail. True, Grinling Gibbons' carvings adorn the cornices, friezes, doorcases and picture frames, especially in the King's staterooms, but there are no marble interiors or exquisite flourishes to compare with the great French palaces. Paintings and tapestries hide bare walls. This is a building rapidly constructed on a tight budget for monarchs with limited powers. Wren pulled out all the stops, however, when he could. The King's staircase, with a wrought-iron balustrade by Jean Tijou, is regal, though Horace Walpole carped at Antonio Verrio's allegorical decoration, claiming the artist painted 'as ill as if he had spoiled it out of principle'. Beyond lie the King's guard chamber – the walls artfully embellished with 3,000 pikes, muskets, pistols, swords and drums – and then an enfilade of dark panelled rooms leading to William III's tiny closet, or private study, where he attended to State business and signed documents.

Wren designed duplicate apartments for the Queen on the opposite side of Fountain Court. These are also approached by a grand staircase and lead to Her Majesty's drawing-room and bedchamber overlooking the Long Water.

A circular maze was planted in the 1690s and was later replaced by the triangular version existing now – half a mile of twists and turns between high hedges, claustrophobic and genuinely perplexing. Like Harris in *Three Men in a Boat*, it is possible to be too confident about a swift exit. The attendants estimate it usually takes visitors about fifteen minutes to find their way out once they have made their way to the heart of the maze. Those who know the secret of the labyrinth, however, can stride confidently to the centre in four minutes and re-emerge just as quickly. The trick on entering is to keep the hedge on your left at all times. When you come to a gap don't cross it, but follow the hedge round. On the way you will go up two blind alleys, but eventually you will reach the centre. To leave, follow the same procedure. Always keep the hedge on your left, cross no openings, proceed up two blind alleys and four minutes later you will arrive at the exit.

In addition to the maze, Tijou beautified the gardens with ornamental ironwork – gates, balustrades and twelve screens at the river end of the Privy Gardens that are universally admired. 'One of the finest works of art at Hampton Court,' exclaimed an editor of *The Times*, Simon Jenkins. 'Grapes ripen, harps play, roses bloom and cherubs dance as if all spun from glass. Tijou could make hard iron break into leaf and burst into flower.'

Wren's East Front. Defoe said Hampton Court
had 'put on new clothes' and was 'one of the
most delightful palaces in Europe'

The King's Staircase, created for William III as the ceremonial entrance to the King's State Rooms. Verrio's painting shows the King in the guise of Alexander being introduced to Hercules

The Long Water, an extraordinary mile-long canal lined by trees,
devised by Charles II – one of five vistas radiating from the Queen's
Apartments at the centre of Wren's Baroque East Front

Wren (who lived in Old Court House on the Green from 1708 until his death in 1723) also laid out the magnificent avenue of horse chestnut trees in Bushy Park, which stretches northwards for a mile from the Lion Gate and was intended to be part of a grand entrance to the palace. Rebuilding at Hampton Court came to a standstill when Mary died of smallpox in 1694, and Wren's far-reaching plans were never realized even though work restarted four years later.

William was overwhelmed by the death of his wife and burdened with ill health. Nonetheless, he insisted on vigorous exercise and often hunted in the park. On Saturday 21 February 1702 he suffered a fatal accident as he was riding. 'While I endeavoured to make the horse change his walking into a gallop,' gasped the King, 'he fell upon his knees … he fell forward to one side, and so I fell with my right shoulder upon the ground. 'Tis a strange thing, for it happened upon smooth level ground.'

The King broke his collar-bone and was carried back to the palace. A fortnight later he died. Tradition says his horse stumbled on a molehill and ever since Jacobites have drunk a toast to the 'little gentleman in black velvet'.

George II was the last monarch to live in Hampton Court, but, hidden away a mile to the north, events were happening in Bushy House. This red brick building, which is now part of the National Physical Laboratory and concealed behind a double barbed-wire fence, heavy foliage and high brick walls, was once the home of Lord North. As George III's Prime Minister for twelve years, he is chiefly remembered for losing Britain's American colonies. 'I will never yield till I have seen America at my feet,' he declared. But North's stern measures after the Boston Tea Party helped unite Americans against Britain and provoked the War of Independence.

Later, Bushy House was occupied by the third son of George III, the Duke of Clarence, who became William IV. Here he lived happily with his mistress, the actress Dorothy Jordan, who bore him ten children. William, known as the 'Sailor King', spent much of his life in the navy and never expected to inherit the throne. He frequently swore, spat on the floor and was called 'Silly Billy' because of his eccentric behaviour. On his accession in 1830, however, he got his own back. While the Privy Council knelt in homage before him he inquired, 'Who's a Silly Billy now?'

Important as the historic figures are who lived in Bushy Park and Hampton Court, none changed the lives of so many people as the modest man who spent his last years in a house a few doors from Sir Christopher Wren's home on Hampton Court Green. The discoveries of the scientist Michael Faraday, the father of electricity, changed the world. By inventing the dynamo and producing electricity from magnetism, he made possible the production of electrical power in vast quantities. He also created the first electric motor and transformer. In recognition of his achievements, Queen Victoria presented him with a house at Hampton Court in 1858 and here he passed away, sitting peacefully in his chair in his study, on 25 August 1867.

Wolsey's coat of arms over the Anne Boleyn Gateway. Made in terracotta and showing his cardinal's hat and motto: Dominus Mihi Adjutor – *God is, or God be, my Judge*

3   The Proud Scene

A huge explosion shook Richmond and Twickenham in January 1772. Three gunpowder-mills blew up on Hounslow Heath with such violence that the explosion was felt in Gloucester. A mile away in Strawberry Hill Horace Walpole, the youngest son of Britain's first Prime Minister, was shaken as his castle windows shattered and statues smashed. 'At London it was proclaimed an earthquake,' he declared, 'and half the inhabitants ran into the street.'

The remains of the Hounslow Powder Mills lie on the River Crane. Gunpowder had been manufactured here since Tudor times, and during the works' Victorian heyday 320 people were employed. It is one of the most extraordinary places in the borough with frothing water surging through narrow creeks, giant mill wheels tossed on the ground, broken walls and earth heaped up in blast hills that surrounded small sheds where the powder was ground. The most intriguing feature is a conical 'Shot Tower' dated 1828, though it is unlikely lead shot was cast here as the tower is too short. Experts think it was used either as a lookout or water tower for fire-fighting or hydraulic equipment. The works closed in 1927 and the area is now a nature reserve, but the ground is wild and broken and trees with their tops blown off are still visible. Explosions were frequent.

Horace Walpole's alarm was shared by thousands of local people, for by 1772 Richmond, Twickenham and the surrounding villages were fast developing. The riverside had become a place of escape when epidemics such as the plague swept London. During the seventeenth and eighteenth centuries nobles, aristocrats and City merchants built splendid houses close to the river and would sail upstream from the City and Westminster to Kew, Richmond, Ham, Petersham, Twickenham and Hampton. They were also attracted by the court. Although the royal family had abandoned the remains of Richmond Palace, the presence of the Hanoverians at Richmond Lodge in the Old Deer Park, Kew, Richmond Park and Hampton Court lured high society up river and in their wake followed the gentry, writers, artists and actors, all of whom left their mark.

A bell on the 'Shot Tower' rang when danger
threatened the mills that produced up to 600
barrels of gunpowder each week

Richmond town was graced with elegant houses on the Green such as Maids of Honour Row (which accommodated the ladies-in-waiting of Caroline, Princess of Wales), Old Palace Terrace, Oak House, Old Palace Place, Old Court House and Old Friars – built on a site adjoining the monastery founded by Henry VII in 1505. A concert hall appeared and in 1766 a new small theatre, whose stage enticed distinguished London actors, including Edmund Kean, William Macready and Mrs Siddons. David Garrick penned the opening prologue and the diarist and biographer of Dr Johnson, James Boswell, recorded a visit in 1769 to the handsome building that had 'everything in miniature'.

In the same year Great Street, which was Richmond's main highway, was re-named George Street to honour George III, who often visited the town and was a genial and popular figure. King Street was also named after him. George III personally provided money to build a workhouse at Pesthouse Common on the lower slopes of the hill, where Grove Road is today. Built in 1786, the workhouse contained cells where tramps earned their keep by breaking up half a ton of stones into pieces small enough to pass through metal grills in the walls. The stones were used for road repairs. Other inmates produced clothes and shoes and did weaving, leatherwork and farming.

Further up the hill homes for the wealthy appeared, including one owned by the King's card-maker, Christopher Blanchard, who built a grand house at No. 3 The Terrace. 'All his cards must have come up trumps,' joked the King one day when riding past.

On the crest Sir William Chambers built Wick House for the first president of the Royal Academy, Sir Joshua Reynolds. The painter used it as a weekend retreat and entertained members of the Literary Club, which included Dr Johnson, James Boswell, Edmund Burke, Edward Gibbon, David Garrick and Oliver Goldsmith. Reynolds' painting of the view from the hill is one of his few landscapes.

A few yards away, at the corner of Nightingale Lane, Robert Mylne designed The Wick for Lady St Aubyn, who occupied one of the most elegant houses in Richmond, subtly decorated and with an oval drawing-room overlooking the view. That view was celebrated in verse by James Thomson, who is best remembered for writing the words for *Rule Britannia*. In his poem *The Seasons* he described the 'matchless vale of Thames' on a summer's day in 1727, the 'boundless landscape', 'smiling meads' with illustrious residents and estates – an Arcadian vision of 'Happy Britannia' that has ever since influenced the way writers and artists perceive the English landscape, particularly the Thames at Richmond.

Thomson lived in a house in Kew Foot Lane and was supported by a pension of £100 a year from Frederick, Prince of Wales. He died in August 1748, was buried in Richmond Parish Church and has a memorial

Richmond Parish Church, a Tudor tower with Georgian additions. Here the actor Edmund Kean, poet James Thomson and Viscount Fitzwilliam lie buried

Ormeley Lodge, Ham Common, where the Prince regent celebrated an illicit honeymoon

The Richmond Workhouse, Pesthouse Common, whose building was paid for by George III

The Twickenham Ferry, now superseded by the nearby Hammerton's, plied for trade with rowing boats from 1640 until the 1980s

in Poets' Corner in Westminster Abbey next to William Shakespeare's.

Meanwhile in Twickenham, Georgian terraces, which might be at home in Westminster, were erected in Montpelier and Sion Rows and the parish church of St Mary the Virgin was rebuilt in a startling manner when the nave collapsed. Retaining the medieval tower, the architect John James added a plain, red brick box. Something similar happened to Richmond parish church, whose Tudor tower acquired a Georgian body.

Wealthy Georgian houses, subtly proportioned and with delicate ironwork, sprang up in Ham and Petersham. They included Ormeley Lodge, which was subsequently enveloped in royal scandal. Petersham's tiny church (St Peter's) was remodelled with a gallery and box pews for which families paid fees. In the churchyard lies the grave of Captain George Vancouver, who circumnavigated the world, sailed with Captain Cook on his last voyage and discovered Vancouver Island in Canada. From 1795 he lived in Glen Cottage, River Lane, but his health was broken and he was only forty when he died in 1798. An annual service of commemoration is held at his graveside each May.

At Barnes houses were constructed by the riverside and the novelist and creator of *Tom Jones*, Henry Fielding, lived in Milbourne House overlooking the pond on the Green, having moved there from a house in Twickenham that has since vanished.

In Mortlake High Street there are more Georgian houses. Regretfully the tapestry works, which had Raphael's cartoons on the premises when Charles I ordered them to be copied, closed in 1703. Set up under James I, they became world famous, but they depended on royal patronage and never recovered from Cromwell's rule.

By the middle of the eighteenth century it was obvious the horse ferry at Richmond could no longer cope with the increasing traffic between the town and the equally fashionable Twickenham. It was also dangerous and unreliable in bad weather. On 12 November 1763 Horace Walpole complained that he was forced to return to the wooden bridge at Kew, 'for the Thames was swelled so violently that the ferry could not work'. A few years later he risked the ferry on a dark, stormy night while the new bridge was still being built: 'The bargemen were drunk, the poles would scarce reach the bottom, and in five minutes the rapidity of the current turned the barge round, and in an instant we were at Isleworth.' Eventually, the bargemen struggled the couple of miles up stream but, 'we ran against the piles of the new bridge, which startled the horses, who began kicking'. Ten minutes later Walpole scrambled ashore.

After years of arguments, a five-arched bridge designed by James Paine and Kenton Couse opened in 1777. There were so many wrangles during construction that no one bothered with an official ceremony. It was left to *The London Magazine* to point out that the architects had designed 'one of the most beautiful ornaments of the river ... and connoisseurs in painting will instantly be reminded of some of the best performances of Claude Lorraine'.

Harmonizing with the landscape and with its gleaming stonework reflected in the water, the bridge remains one of the most urbane crossings on the Thames, for the architects did more than solve a practical problem: they produced a symbol of Richmond to complement the great houses and villas on the riverbanks between Kew and Hampton.

York House in Twickenham was acquired by the Earl of Clarendon after the Restoration when Charles II occupied Hampton Court. The Earl had introduced the Clarendon Code to ensure the supremacy of the Church of England. Historians dispute if he stayed in York House, but he did live in Twickenham. Meanwhile, across the water lies one of Britain's best preserved seventeenth-century buildings: Ham House, occupied by another of Charles' ministers, the Earl of Lauderdale. He was one of the King's five closest advisers, known as 'the Cabal' from the first letters of their names. They met frequently in the house and at weekends it was claimed that 'all England was ruled from Petersham'.

Ham House originally had been built in 1610 for one of James I's courtiers and was later owned by Elizabeth, Countess of Dysart, who married Lauderdale in St Peter's church. The Earl was ambitious, learned and possessed a remarkable memory, but he was ruthless and had a vile temper. The House of Commons tried unsuccessfully to ban him from the King's presence.

Ham House is virtually unchanged since 1670, and the visitor who steps through the door enters the world of Charles II. Lauderdale and his equally ambitious and dominating wife poured money into their home, converting it into a small palace with a marble entrance hall, carved staircase and sumptuously decorated rooms, hung with tapestries and delicate silk hangings. It was 'inferior to few of the best villas in Italy', observed John Evelyn when he visited Ham in 1678. 'The house was furnished like a great prince's.'

A severe fire damaged the building in 1721. Daniel Defoe reported the blaze was 'so sudden, and so furious, that the family who were all at home, had scarce time to save their lives.' Rich furniture, paintings and the library were 'wholly consumed'. Ham House took two centuries to recover and was eventually restored by the National Trust. Amid the splendours is a piquant curiosity. Carefully preserved in a cabinet of miniatures is a lock of hair said to have been cut from the head of Elizabeth's favourite, the Earl of Essex, on the morning of his execution in the Tower of London.

On the opposite bank of the river stands Marble Hill House, a cool, classical villa created for Henrietta Howard, mistress of George II and later Countess of Suffolk. This delightful Palladian mansion designed by

Richmond Bridge, the oldest on London's river,
opened in 1777. It was painted by Rowlandson
and Turner and admired by Henry James

The Cloisters, Ham House – 'the sleeping beauty among country houses', where time has stood still since Charles II's reign

The magnificent riverside gardens of York House were once private property, but are now open to all.

Henry, Lord Herbert and built between 1724–9 by Roger Morris, breathes the spirit of the Augustan Age. Inside all is poise and decorum. A grand carved mahogany staircase sweeps up to the first floor and the glory of the house, the Great Room – a twenty-four foot cube decorated in white and gold, with gilded cherubs over the chimneypiece. The room apparently has four entrances, but two doors are false and were inserted for symmetry.

Marble Hill attracted wits and writers, including Jonathan Swift and John Gay. Horace Walpole, a friend and frequent visitor, spent two hours with Lady Suffolk the day before she died at the age of seventy-nine in the summer of 1767. Another guest, the poet Alexander Pope who lived a mile upstream, helped plan the park.

Pope was thirty and already famous when he moved to Twickenham in 1719, having published *An Essay on Criticism* and *The Rape of the Lock*. As a Catholic he was barred by law from owning a property in London. The money he earned from his translation of Homer's *Iliad*, however, enabled him to acquire a villa at Twickenham, which he called 'Twitnam'. At that time the parish had a population of about 1500 and his friend, the society hostess Lady Mary Wortley Montagu, maintained there 'was more company than in London'. She lived here in summer and claimed, 'Twickenham is become so fashionable and the neighbourhood so enlarged that it is more like Tunbridge or Bath than a country retreat.'

Pope's villa was separated from the river by a road, under which ran a tunnel. This the poet converted into a grotto, decorating the walls with sparkling shells, stones, and mirrors. Peering through the grotto at one end he could see 'the sails on the river passing suddenly and vanishing as thro' a perspective glass'. Shut the doors and it was transformed from a luminous room into a camera obscura, 'on the walls of which all objects of the river, hills, woods and boats, are forming a moving picture in their visible radiations'.

Dr Johnson scoffed at the grotto and declared it 'frivolous and childish'. But to Pope it was a place of enchantment where he wrote many of his most memorable lines. The grotto and garden he created were a private world where he could escape from the painful reality of his life, for Pope was a crippled hunchback, just four feet six inches tall. Splenetic and quarrelsome because of his illnesses, he made many enemies, earning the epithet of 'the Wasp of Twickenham'.

In September 1726 Pope narrowly escaped death late one night when a coach bringing him home overturned and fell into the nearby River Crane. Water poured in 'up to the knots of his periwig' and he nearly drowned. Voltaire, who had recently fled to England from France, wrote a letter of condolence and arrived at Twickenham, but his conversation was so unbridled that Pope's mother fled from the dinner table in

A Palladian villa for a king's mistress. Marble Hill was built by Henrietta Howard with £11,500 provided by her lover George II

*Pope's Grotto, all that remains from the poet's fantasy at Twickenham.
His elegant riverside garden and house have long gone*

*The Thames between Pope's Grotto and Strawberry
Hill – 'one of the most influential landscapes in the
history of the English Landscape Movement'.*

disgust. In the same year Swift stayed several weeks but was so distressed by Pope's afflictions that he departed, leaving the poet distraught. Pope wrote in anguish, saying he could not see 'one seat in my own garden, or one room in my own house, without a phantom of you, sitting or walking before me'.

Pope created a kingdom of the mind on the banks of the Thames. Here he lived with his mother and nurse. As he got older, walking became impossible and he was carried around in a sedan-chair. In his final days he sat in the garden he loved and just before he died went for an airing in Bushy Park. He passed away the following evening, on 30 May 1744, and was buried in Twickenham parish church.

Today only his grotto survives. Stone dogs that once ornamented the garden now guard one end of the long, dark tunnel beneath the road, while the river entrance is sealed off by iron gates. The magic has gone. A later owner, infuriated by pilgrims who came to see the poet's home, tore down the building and now a convent school stands in its place.

Pope's villa had been designed by James Gibbs, who built the Radcliffe Camera in Oxford and St Martin-in-the-Fields in Trafalgar Square. Two of his buildings still exist in the borough – in Petersham, Sudbrook Park, with its fine Baroque cube room, built for the Duke of Argyll; and in Twickenham the Octagon or garden room, which belonged to Orleans House, where Queen Caroline was entertained and where, a hundred years later, Louis-Philippe, King of the French, lived in exile. Downstream, within sight of Richmond Bridge, Sir Robert Taylor designed a superb Palladian villa, Asgill House, for a Lord Mayor of London.

Three years after Pope died Horace Walpole bought a cottage close to the Thames on the outskirts of Twickenham at Strawberry Hill. Walpole was thirty when he acquired 'a little plaything house … the prettiest bauble you ever saw … set in enamelled meadows, with filigree hedges'.

With the help of ten architects he transformed the building into a Gothic fantasy with turrets, battlements, a round tower, gloomy arches, heraldic glass, gilded canopies, niches filled with saints and old trophies, a staircase with suits of armour and a chapel in the woods. The building wasn't so much designed as assembled from medieval fragments, like an ancient architectural jig-saw puzzle. 'All Gothic designs,' Walpole observed, 'should be made to imitate something that was at that time, a part of church, a castle, a convent, or a mansion.' So he recruited a small group of friends as advisers, called 'The Committee of Taste', and together they culled ideas from venerable buildings and books in Walpole's library. A medieval tomb became a fireplace, while a screen from old St Paul's was transformed into an elaborate Gothic bookcase.

The Round Drawing-Room contained a chimneypiece inspired by Edward the Confessor's tomb in Westminster Abbey, but 'improved' by

James Gibbs's Octagon Room – the only surviving
part of Orleans House where Queen Caroline was
entertained and Louis-Philipe lived in exile

Robert Adam. In the Holbein Chamber the grand chimneypiece combined features from the high altar in Rouen Cathedral and Archbishop Warham's tomb at Canterbury. The ribbed ceiling resembled the Queen's dressing-room at Windsor and the fretted screen eighteenth-century choir gates.

It was in the Holbein Chamber that Walpole had the nightmare that inspired him to write the first Gothic novel, *The Castle of Otranto*. He had dreamed he was in an ancient castle when he saw on the bannister of a great staircase 'a gigantic hand in armour'. That same evening he began writing and in less than two months completed the book. Filled with supernatural happenings, trap doors, miraculous events, ghosts, terror and catastrophes, it became a best-seller and has inspired horror stories ever since. 'I gave rein to my imagination,' he confessed. 'Visions and passions choked me.'

Some scenes in the novel were set in Strawberry Hill, where the most fantastic room, the Gallery, has a papier mâché ceiling copied from the fan-vaulting of Henry VII's chapel in Westminster Abbey. The walls are covered with crimson damask, gilt fretwork and reflecting glass. Below lie the cloisters.

Pedants were outraged. 'A ginger-bread castle,' they sneered, 'a grotesque house with pie-crust battlements.' Strawberry Hill wasn't really Gothic; it was a sham. Indeed, by constructing his castle out of materials different from the originals – a 'romance in lath and plaster' he called it – Walpole altered its character, making it genteel, stagy and rococo. But Strawberry Hill was a delight and outdistanced its critics. Society, including royalty, flocked to see it. The crowning moment came in June 1766 when George III and his Queen spent two hours exploring the castle. 'They were exceedingly pleased with it,' wrote the elated owner, 'and the Queen so much that she said she would come again.'

Despite seductions, life at Strawberry Hill had awkward moments. In 1755 there were floods – 'The whole lawn was a lake … it drowned the pretty blue bed-chamber, passed through ceilings and floor … You never saw such desolation!' The castle was raided by burglars. And in October 1781 Walpole had his carriage stopped by a highwayman while riding through Twickenham Park and was robbed of his purse and nine guineas. 'I cannot now stir a mile from my own house after sunset,' he wrote later, 'without one or two servants with blunderbusses.'

Nonetheless, Walpole usually led a tranquil existence. He established a printing press and the vast quantity of letters he wrote from his castle give one of the finest pictures of eighteenth-century upper-class society and contemporary taste. Strawberry Hill was the most influential of the early Gothic Revival buildings and subsequent Victorian additions by Lady Waldegrave, though less inspired, did little to detract from the original.

'I am going to build a little Gothic castle,' said
Horace Walpole. The result, Strawberry Hill, a
key influence in the Gothic Revival

Walpole acquired a new neighbour in 1754 when the greatest actor of the day, David Garrick, moved into a villa near the river at Hampton. The Adam Brothers made extensive alterations, adding a wooden-columned portico and orangery, while 'Capability' Brown laid out the grounds with serpentine walks and enticing vistas.

At the water's edge Garrick built an octagonal temple with a domed roof and large windows in honour of his idol Shakespeare. This housed relics that were said to have belonged to the Bard – his gloves, a signet ring engraved with the initials W.S. and a chair made from a mulberry tree that the poet was reputed to have planted. Pride of place went to a statue of Shakespeare, carved by Roubiliac, which was modelled on Garrick. Guests were encouraged to write verses in praise of the poet and lay them at the foot of the monument.

The temple had one disadvantage – it was cut off from Hampton House by a road. So, like Alexander Pope, Garrick created a tunnel similar to a grotto, at one end of which was a bath-house. Visitors were enchanted: 'The dazzling silver flood of the Thames,' wrote the biographer Carola Oman, 'on a day of blue skies through the dripping black grotto arch, in which voices echoed weirdly, was highly dramatic, and emerging from it on to the Temple Lawn was like stepping into fairyland.' Children used to stand there throwing their hats at swallows darting through the tunnel.

The temple was the hub of social gatherings. Garrick enjoyed picnicking with his family and wining and dining his friends, entertaining on a grand scale. In the summer of 1774 he and his wife celebrated their silver wedding with a huge party, which included a concert lit by 6,000 coloured lamps, followed by fireworks.

The scene was idyllic with swans and wild ducks and boats drifting past on the smooth waters. Here Garrick could fish and relax, or sit in the temple learning the lines for his next play. Robert Adam taught him golf and on one occasion a guest excited applause by hitting a ball through the tunnel and into the river in two strokes. Garrick asked to keep the club as a memento.

Like Strawberry Hill, Hampton House attracted the fashionable – the King of Denmark, the nobility, bishops and theatrical and literary celebrities. The notorious MP John Wilkes, who called himself the 'friend of liberty' and was a member of the Hell Fire Club, turned up one day expecting hospitality. Zoffany painted Mr and Mrs Garrick on the lawn and Dr Johnson, who published his dictionary in 1755, was a frequent, though untidy, visitor. He caused dismay when he ripped Garrick's books from the shelves, glanced at their contents and tossed them on the floor. Nonetheless, he was made welcome and when asked if he liked the villa replied, 'Ah, David, it is the leaving of such a place that makes a death-bed terrible.'

Papier mâché magnificence – the Gothic splendours of Henry VII's chapel in Westminster Abbey recreated in Strawberry Hill's Long Gallery.

Unlike Walpole, Garrick was no snob. He played an active part in the local community. Each year he invited poor children from the village to a party on Temple Lawn. Garrick sat on the mulberry chair beside Shakespeare's statue while the children were led up one by one to receive a shilling and a piece of plum cake.

His marriage to the actress Eva Maria Veigel was exceptionally happy. The religious writer Hannah More, who wrote two tragedies for Garrick, remembered the couple 'laughing over their tea under their walnut-tree'. When Garrick died in 1779 his widow lived in the house until her death forty-three years later. The villa still exists, along with the temple and the tunnel beneath the road, though Roubiliac's statue is now in the British Museum.

Despite distinguished inhabitants, by the end of the eighteenth century Richmond was only a small town with about 4,500 inhabitants and Twickenham a large village. Barnes, Mortlake, Kew, Petersham, Hampton and Teddington were little more than hamlets. Scandalous events could happen without stirring up the local community. In 1795 the Prince of Wales' mistress, Mrs Maria Fitzherbert, lived at Marble Hill. Mrs Fitzherbert, a Catholic whose two husbands had died, had been besieged ten years before by the Prince, who later became Prince Regent and George IV. As a teenager he showed a huge appetite for women and in his twenties ran up vast debts and fell passionately in love with Mrs Fitzherbert, whom he blackmailed into marrying him by threats of suicide.

The couple were secretly married without George III's consent on 15 December 1785 and in flagrant defiance of Parliament, whose laws excluded anyone who married a Catholic from inheriting the throne. The ceremony was performed in Mrs Fitzherbert's London home by a disreputable clergyman, the Revd. Robert Burt, who became vicar of Twickenham. He was in prison for debt and agreed to conduct the wedding if he were paid £500 to settle with his creditors. Burt also insisted on being made one of the Prince's chaplains and later a bishop. After the ceremony the couple set off for a week's honeymoon at Ormeley Lodge, Ham Common, where they arrived in deep snow.

The Prince's behaviour damaged the monarchy and may have contributed towards the King's breakdown at Windsor three years later. Much against his will, the King was persuaded to come to Kew, where the royal family had their country homes. Here he was subjected to barbarous medical treatment, while the country was plunged into a constitutional crisis.

David Garrick's Temple to Shakespeare erected in 1755 in his riverside garden at Hampton. Here the famous actor studied his lines and entertained fashionable society, as well as organizing parties for local children. The garden, now open to the public, is known as Garrick's Lawn

4 Royal Kew

A hundred yards from the Dutch House and the Orangery at the northern end of Kew Gardens stands a sundial. An inscription tells visitors that a telescope once stood on the site, enabling the Revd. James Bradley (who later became Astronomer-Royal) to discover 'the aberration of light and the nutation of the earth's axis'. The telescope, says the inscription, was erected 'in a house which afterwards became a royal residence and was taken down in 1803'. The carefully incised words fail, however, to record a more sinister event, for the sundial marks the position of the White House where George III suffered from an illness that drove him to madness.

During the eighteenth century Kew became a favourite retreat for the royal family, who took over and enlarged the existing buildings and transformed the gardens. Courtiers, including Elizabeth I's Earl of Leicester, had occupied houses in the area since Tudor times so they could be near the monarch. And John Evelyn recorded in his diary on 27 August 1678 a visit to Sir Henry Capel's old timber house at Kew, whose garden had 'the choicest fruits of any plantation in England'.

About a mile away in the Old Deer Park lay Richmond Lodge, the home of George II and Queen Caroline. Here, on 14 June 1727, George heard he had become King. He was asleep after dinner when the Prime Minister, Sir Robert Walpole, burst into his bedroom, woke him and told him the news. 'Dat is one big lie!' roared the King in a strong German accent. And he started up from his bed 'with many oaths', for he was suspicious that his father had tried to trick him.

Later, George II's estranged son Frederick, Prince of Wales, occupied Sir Henry Capel's home which William Kent converted into a Palladian mansion renamed the White House.

The heir to the throne was the first member of the royal family to become an enthusiastic cricketer, the *London Post* reporting in 1737: 'On Thursday morning, July 13th, His Royal Highness the Prince of Wales and ten gentlemen play'd a match of cricket at Kew for a considerable sum against His Grace the Duke of Marlborough and ten other noblemen and gentlemen, which was won by His Royal Highness.'

The Palm House and pond, focal points in the
Royal Botanic Gardens which contain the world's
most comprehensive collection of living plants

Regarded by many as stupid (he was called 'Poor Fred'), the Prince nonetheless took an intelligent interest in the arts, played the cello and was a connoisseur of painting, buying five Van Dycks and Rubens' landscapes. He cultivated the friendship of eminent artists and writers, including Alexander Pope. The poet returned the compliment by presenting the Prince with a pet dog on whose collar was engraved the famous verse: 'I am his Highness' dog at Kew; / Pray tell me, sir, whose dog are you?'

The Prince enriched and beautified the White House gardens, encouraged by John Stuart, Earl of Bute, who lived on Kew Green and was an enthusiastic botanist. They first met in 1747, Bute prompting Frederick to import exotic plants from abroad and plan a 300-foot-long greenhouse. But while walking at Kew on a cold spring day in 1751, Frederick caught a chill and died. The impetus he gave to the botanic gardens was continued, however, by his widow, Princess Augusta. She laid out a nine-acre botanic garden in 1759, the nucleus of today's science and pleasure gardens. Lord Bute continued advising and employed the gardener William Aiton to improve the grounds. Meanwhile, Sir William Chambers, who designed Somerset House, adorned Kew with temples, follies, a ruined arch, the Wren-like Orangery and the first pagoda in Europe.

As a young man Chambers had visited China and by the mid-eighteenth century Chinoiserie was in vogue. His Pagoda, built in only six months in 1761 for Princess Augusta, soon loomed above the trees. This Georgian skyscraper – ten storeys and 163 feet high – excited wonder and was visible nearly two miles away. 'We begin to perceive the tower at Kew from Montpelier Row,' wrote an astonished Horace Walpole. 'In a fortnight you will see it from Yorkshire.' Eighty brilliantly coloured dragons glittered on the roofs, decorated with glazed tiles and bells.

Chambers also served as architectural tutor to the future George III who, when he was King, joined the two royal estates together – hence the title Royal Botanic Gardens. They formed just over 300 acres and still exist today.

Most school children remember George III as the 'Mad King' who said 'What! What!', lost the American colonies and was condemned in the Declaration of Independence as despotic and 'unfit to be the ruler of a free people'. As a young man he fell under the spell of his tutor, Lord Bute, whom he idolized and made Prime Minister in 1762, replacing the popular Pitt and transforming Bute into the most hated politician in the country.

Although politically inept, George III had many attributes; he was diligent, pious and cultured. Bute stimulated his interest in agriculture and the King ran a local farm from which sheep were sold to Australia

The Great Pagoda, Kew's best-known landmark
and one of two dozen exotic buildings Sir
William Chambers designed for the gardens

where they helped found a huge industry. The King also wrote pamphlets on agriculture under the pen name of Ralph Robinson.

In addition, George III developed a lifelong enthusiasm for astronomy, inviting Sir William Chambers in 1769 to build an observatory in the Old Deer Park, where he could watch the transit of Venus and calculate the distance of the Earth from the Sun. There the King established his own workshops and kept a collection of clocks and watches. For many years London's official time was set at Kew. Sometimes the King himself made observations of the sun passing the meridian, by which clocks in Parliament, the Horse Guards and Whitehall were regulated, pre-dating Greenwich.

George III was one of the first British monarchs to separate his official and home life. Buckingham House was his London home, St James's his place of business, but he was happiest surrounded by his family at Windsor and Kew. Much of his boyhood was spent in the White House and on the death of his mother in 1772 he made it a summer residence. The King lived a surprisingly middle-class life, without pomp or splendour. He rose at six in the morning and would knock on his children's doors, asking if they'd had a good night's sleep. The White House soon proved too small, though, for the King and Queen had fifteen children – the largest family in the history of the British monarchy. As their family expanded they took over houses on the Green and occupied the nearby Dutch House (now Kew Palace), built in 1631 for a rich London merchant of Dutch descent. Here, in England's smallest royal palace, the Prince of Wales (later Prince Regent and George IV) and his brother Frederick were brought up in a 'miniature academy' and a household independent from their parents. On display now are George IV's high chair, comfortably cushioned in red velvet, his silver filigree rattle, alphabetical counters carved from ivory by which he learnt to spell and an example of the young Prince's handwriting when he was five – neat copperplate. Discipline was strict and the royal children worked at their lessons from early in the morning until eight at night. One of their sisters recalled seeing the two boys 'held by their tutors to be flogged like dogs with a long whip'.

While at Kew the Prince of Wales was involved in a curious incident with a gardener. A young man in his teens had heard of the beauties of Kew and one summer's day walked there from his home town of Farnham in Surrey. Arriving in Richmond he spent his last pence on a copy of Swift's *Tale of a Tub*, then made his way to Kew Gardens where he sat down to read under the shade of a haystack. He fell asleep and next morning was offered a job by a gardener. The young man was William Cobbett, who became a radical journalist, social reformer and author of *Rural Rides*. As a teenager he wore a blue smock and red garters tied at the knees. On one occasion, while sweeping the grass round the

Kew Palace (the Dutch House), Kew's oldest building and a home for George III, Queen Charlotte and the young Prince Regent

base of the Pagoda, he was spotted by the Prince of Wales and two of his brothers who laughed at the oddness of his dress. Cobbett was incensed and later in life when he was famous, attacked the Prince for his politics and outrageous behaviour.

The Prince, unfortunately, gained little moral benefit from his education and found life stifling at Kew. Soon he was involved in scandal and up to his ears in debt. Worse still, he allied himself with the Whig opposition in Parliament, flouting the King and government.

In October 1788 disaster struck. While the King was at Windsor he had convulsions and began talking gibberish. A few weeks later he attacked the Prince of Wales and tried to smash his head against a wall. After much persuasion the King was induced to move to Kew. When he arrived at the White House he was in acute pain. From his lips poured a torrent of obscenities; he was violent and uncontrollable and in a furious rage lashed out at his servants, punching one, pulling another by the hair and kicking a third. Foam dribbled from his mouth and a cloudy mist floated before his eyes.

Francis Willis, a clergyman specializing in madness, was called in. He believed the way to handle the mentally ill was to 'break in' a patient like a horse. The King took an instant dislike to him.

'Sir,' protested Dr Willis, 'Our Saviour himself went about healing the sick.'

'Yes, yes,' snapped the King, 'but he had not £700 a year for it.'

News of the monarch's illness caused panic on the Stock Market and a political crisis. The government drew up a Regency Bill and there was fear that the Prince of Wales might take power.

Meanwhile, there were extraordinary scenes in Kew. As the White House was freezing in winter, sandbags were stacked round the ill-fitting doors and windows to keep out the draughts. The King was tied to his bed and confined to a straitjacket, or strapped into an iron chair, while Dr Willis lectured and threatened him. Blisters were applied to his body to draw out 'evil humours' and large doses of medicines, which made him vomit, poured down his throat.

Occasionally, the King was allowed out in the gardens. On 19 January he and his doctors walked to the Pagoda. The King insisted on climbing to the top, but the door was locked. A page produced the key, whereupon the King grabbed it and a tussle ensued. After a struggle the key was wrested from him and the enraged King sat down on the ground, then sprawled flat out on the grass and refused to move. Eventually he was taken up by force, carried back a mile on his attendants' shoulders and once in the White House strapped in a straitjacket.

Modern doctors have suggested that George III wasn't mad, but suffering from a rare metabolic disorder, porphyria, that produces

The King's Observatory, Old Deer Park, built on the site of a monastery in 1769 so George III could study the heavens.

mental derangement. Gradually the King recovered and local people – indeed the whole nation – rejoiced while the inmates at his new workhouse on Pesthouse Common celebrated with 'legs and shoulders of mutton and a pint of strong beer each for dinner'. During his convalescence the King visited them and the Master of the workhouse proudly showed his royal guest the lunatic wing where the mentally ill were trussed up in straitjackets. The King regarded this alarming sight with surprising equanimity.

Life returned to normal at Kew and the White House was eventually demolished. The King and Queen moved into the Dutch House as a temporary measure while a vast new palace was constructed nearby, but it was never completed and was later pulled down.

The Dutch House was George III's and Queen Charlotte's country home from 1802 and remained in royal occupation until Charlotte's death in 1818. The building incorporates fittings rescued from the White House – wall panelling and beautifully crafted brass door locks engraved with the initials and badge of Frederick, Prince of Wales.

George III lived a simple life at Kew like a country gentleman and often went for walks without an equerry. Henry Addington, who was briefly Prime Minister, dined with the King at the Dutch House in 1805. He was about to be created Viscount Sidmouth and was surprised to find lunch 'consisting of mutton-chops and pudding'.

In July 1818 the white and gold drawing-room was the scene of the double wedding of the Duke of Clarence (later William IV) and Queen Victoria's father, the Duke of Kent, watched by Queen Charlotte in a wheelchair. After the ceremony the royal party made their way to the Queen's cottage in the southwest corner of the gardens where the Prince Regent had organized tea. Although this thatched-roofed picnic lodge looks simple outside, its interior is elaborate. A curved ceiling adorns the first-floor picnic-room, which is painted leaf green and decorated with flowers. Here the royal family not only enjoyed tea, but sometimes breakfast and dinner.

During George III's reign Sir Joseph Banks became the unofficial director of the Botanic Gardens and collectors were sent all over the world to find plants. Banks was taken on his first voyage to the South Seas by Captain James Cook who discovered Botany Bay. Another voyage sponsored by the King involved *HMS Bounty* and Captain William Bligh, who provoked the famous mutiny. Four years later Bligh was more successful and the Kew Records Book for 1793 reports he returned to Kew with numerous plants, including cocoa.

After George III's death the botanic gardens declined and in 1840 were handed over to the state. The next year Sir William Hooker was appointed the first official director. During Queen Victoria's reign Kew became 'The Wonder Garden of the Empire'. Between 1844 and 1848 the

The Temperate House by Decimus Burton – the largest glass house at Kew – protects endangered plants from warmer and sub-tropical climates

*A Victorian wonder, the Palm House, stands at the hub of a series of
dramatic vistas. Of novel design it was built from curved metal beams,
like an iron steamship*

A tropical rain forest thrives inside the Palm House, which is 362 feet long, 100 feet wide and 66 feet high. Galleries enable visitors to view the jungle from above

architect Decimus Burton and the engineer Richard Turner built a masterpiece in glass and iron – the Palm House – that excites superlatives from architectural critics. 'How on earth can I convey the utter originality and unselfconscious perfection of this building ... one of the few completely original buildings in the whole of architecture,' exclaimed Ian Nairn. Gavin Stamp savoured the 'beautiful curved surfaces which seem almost to defy gravity and float like glass bubbles'. To Nikolaus Pevsner it was 'one of the boldest pieces of nineteenth-century functionalism in existence'.

Inside, amid steam and mist, flourishes a tropical rain forest – palms, sugar cane, bananas, cocoa, coffee and rubber. In fact the great rubber industries in Sri Lanka and Malaysia were started with plants supplied from Kew.

Half a mile away lies Kew's largest conservatory, the Temperate House, also by Decimus Burton, where subtropical plants are cultivated, including a Chilean wine pine over fifty feet high that threatens to grow through the roof.

Visitors admire the gardens, but scientific work behind the scenes is more important, for Kew is an encyclopedia of the earth's plants – living and dead. One in eight of all species of flowering plants grow here, making the botanical gardens the world's largest collection. Kew also conserves thousands of endangered species. During Victorian times the Herbarium was set up and now contains the world's largest collection of dried plants and fungi – over 6,000,000.

A spectacular new conservatory opened by the Princess of Wales in 1987 contains ten climatic zones, with habitats ranging from desert to mangrove swamp. Here grows the giant Amazonian waterlily (*Victoria amazonica*) whose leaves can measure over six feet in diameter.

The development of Kew village on the Green was directly influenced by the royal presence. Queen Anne granted a plot of land there in 1714 for the parish church (St Anne's) where the painters Gainsborough and Zoffany are buried. As the royal village expanded, the church was unable to accommodate members of the household, so George III had the building enlarged. A royal gallery standing on cast iron columns was added for the King's family and the court. Later, George IV presented an organ to the church which was enlarged still further.

George III's palace guard occupied houses Nos. 2–4 on the Green, while Lord Bute had his library in No. 33 and a residence at No. 37. The latter became the home of the Commander-in-Chief of the British Army, the Duke of Cambridge. Queen Victoria's 'wicked uncle', the Duke of Cumberland, lived in the building that is now the Herbarium. Cosmo Gordon Lang, the Archbishop of Canterbury who presided over Edward VIII's abdication in 1936, lived in King's Cottage opposite St Anne's church. He strongly disapproved of Edward VIII and was so stern it was

The Princess of Wales Conservatory houses
Victoria amazonica, *a giant waterlily with six foot leaves that can support the weight of a baby*

said that men nearly fainted after an interview with him. He crowned George VI and Queen Elizabeth and christened Elizabeth II.

Kew remained largely unchanged until the coming of the railway in 1869. Then, long rows of wistful Victorian and Edwardian houses were laid out between Kew and Richmond, transforming the countryside into a modern suburb. Even on the brightest day a Sunday afternoon melacholy clings to the neighbourhood, a deathly stillness, as if George III's tribulations had seeped into the grounds and surrounding streets.

Regrettably, one of the most extravagant examples of nautical graffiti has long since disappeared. During the Napoleonic wars a disabled sailor drew pictures of the entire British fleet on the boundary wall separating the gardens from Kew Road – 800 ships, each five or six feet long, surmounted by the name of the vessel and the number of guns each carried. The picture stretched for about a mile and a half, but was drawn in chalk and eventually vanished.

Another curio from the age of sail surprised visitors to Station Parade in the 1960s – a wooden figurehead from a nineteenth-century ship. This bare-breasted apparition, staring imperiously into the distance, was fixed above the entrance to an antique shop and loomed over passers-by. Alas, it too has gone.

The ship's figurehead that graced Kew
for thirty years

Kew Parish Church, where Gains-
borough and Zoffany are buried

5 Richmond Park

Six weeks before the Battle of Trafalgar, Admiral Lord Nelson drove over to White Lodge near the centre of Richmond Park. The victor of Cape St Vincent, Copenhagen and the Nile was about to set sail on his final voyage. Aware that he might die in battle, Nelson had come to say farewell to his friend and former Prime Minister Lord Sidmouth, who was unwell. 'On Tuesday forenoon, if superior powers do not prevent me, I will be in Richmond Park,' he wrote on Sunday, 8 September 1805, 'and shall be glad to take you by the hand, and to wish you the most perfect restoration to health.'

Nelson himself looked frail and battered. A national hero, he had already sacrificed one eye and an arm in his country's service. He arrived alone at White Lodge, rain spattering down as his carriage crunched up the gravel drive. The admiral spent some hours with his friend. During conversation in the dining-room he dipped his finger in wine and sketched out on a table his plan for a great naval battle. 'Rodney broke the line in one point,' he declared. 'I will break it in two.'

Subsequently a brass plate was fixed to the centre of the table to commemorate the incident: 'On the 10th day of September, 1805, Vice-Admiral Lord Viscount Nelson described to Lord Sidmouth, upon this table, the manner in which he intended to engage the combined fleets of France and Spain, which he expected shortly to meet. He stated that he would attack them in two lines, led by himself and Admiral Collingwood, and felt confident that he should capture either their van, or their centre and rear ...' This he successfully did at Trafalgar on 21 October 1805, the victory ensuring Britain's dominance of the seas for a century and the safety of her empire. But in the moment of triumph Nelson was shot dead by a sniper's bullet.

The table is preserved in the Sidmouth's West Country home while the White Lodge dining-room, now called the Nelson Room, still retains its eighteenth-century plaster ceiling and panelling.

The history of the house began nearly a century earlier in 1727. During the last year of George I's reign the builder of Marble Hill, Roger Morris, was asked to design a hunting-box for the King – 'a place of refreshment

White Lodge, once the home of royalty and a
prime minister and which a Tsar visited, now
accommodates the Royal Ballet School

after the fatigues of the chase'. He built a Palladian mansion of white Portland stone – hence the name White Lodge – first occupied by George II and his Consort Queen Caroline.

The house stands in the deer park created in 1637 by Charles I who, despite public protests, insisted on buying up private estates and fields and surrounding 2,470 acres of land with a ten-mile wall. The King created London's largest royal park – two and half miles across from north to south and from east to west. Known first as Richmond New Park and later as Richmond Park, this hunting ground was used by royalty and the nobility until the middle of the nineteenth century.

Queen Caroline delighted in White Lodge and each Sunday in summer took tea in the drawing-room with the King. Their monogram is still visible on the fireplace. Her Majesty enjoyed riding on horseback in the park and the broad oak-lined avenue, which runs a mile westward from the back of the lodge, was named Queen's Ride in her honour. She strongly supported Britain's first Prime Minister, Sir Robert Walpole, who made his weekend home a few hundred yards away to the southwest in Old Lodge. He claimed he could do more work in the seclusion of Richmond Park than he could in town and the closing of Parliament on Saturdays dates from this time. Walpole enjoyed hunting, spent large sums of money draining and improving the park and built gates and lodges round the perimeter to keep out the riff-raff.

The King's youngest daughter, Princess Amelia, imposed even stricter measures. From the moment she became ranger or principal officer of the park in 1751, she regarded the land as her private domain. Local people were locked out and forbidden to enter. Petitions and pleas were of no avail. Crowds interfered with the hunting she haughtily declared. After the dispute had gone on for three years a Richmond brewer, John Lewis, took the matter to court. The Princess was ordered to erect ladder-stiles over the walls so ordinary people could climb in. The Princess countered by building stiles with such widely-spaced steps they were impossible to scale. Lewis complained to one of the justices, who ordered that the stiles should be altered. The Princess was forced to give way and angrily departed for Gunnersbury on the other side of the Thames.

The Third Earl of Bute (Prime Minister from 1762–3) and George III afterwards became rangers and from 1801–44 Viscount Sidmouth occupied White Lodge. While here he entertained Sheridan, the younger Pitt and Sir Walter Scott. Enchanted by the setting, the novelist featured it in *The Heart of Midlothian* as well as praising the nearby view from Richmond Hill.

After Lord Sidmouth died – he was buried in St Mary's church, Mortlake – White Lodge became a royal home for the next century. From May to November 1858 the house was almost a prison for the teenage Albert Edward, Prince of Wales. Queen Victoria and Prince Albert were

Royal deer, which have grazed in Richmond Park for centuries, are often seen drinking and washing at the Barn Wood Pond

worried about their elder son. Hard work and a tightly scheduled life left Bertie exhausted and hostile to learning, and he exploded in furious rages. His parents hoped isolation under the eyes of his tutors and carefully regulated company might improve him. The Prince would study music, fine art, poetry and improving books and read aloud good plays.

'Bertie is charmingly established,' enthused the Queen in her diary when she visited the lodge in May. She liked the small rooms, the quiet and the countryside and 'walked about in the lovely small pleasure ground, full of pretty trees & shrubs, the lilacs in fullest blossom, perfuming the air'.

What beguiled a mother, however, failed to enthral her son, who preferred the attractions of society. To relieve the monotony the Prince used to row along the river from Richmond or Mortlake at sundown and visit his aunt, the Duchess of Cambridge, at Kew.

The pressure proved too much. The Prince disliked his tutors, found Sir Walter Scott's novels unreadable and was out of his depth when talking to men of distinction such as the Liberal statesman Lord John Russell. After six months Bertie returned to London. When he was King he told his adviser Lord Esher that 'he hated the memory of White Lodge'.

Three years after his incarceration a grief-stricken Queen Victoria came to the house following the death of her mother, the Duchess of Kent. During their fortnight's stay in May 1861, the Queen and Prince Albert used to walk in the park and go for drives. 'All would be so pleasant,' wrote the Queen, 'were it not for the dreadful reality which constantly breaks upon my mind of my fearful loss.' Despair induced a mental breakdown. She used to sit in the Long Gallery with Albert, reading her mother's papers. The Queen and the Duchess had been estranged for years, but the records revealed a loving parent and caused her anguish – 'little books with accounts of my babyhood and they shew *such* unbounded tenderness! Oh, I am so wretched to think *how for a time* two people most wickedly estranged us … I *dare* not think of it – it drives me *wild* now.'

Despite unhappy memories the Prince of Wales returned with his wife to White Lodge, which in 1867–8 served them as a weekend retreat. Afterwards the Duke and Duchess of Teck lived here with their daughter Mary, the future Consort of George V and mother of two kings. As a youngster, however, Princess May, as she was then called, was much like other girls. She climbed trees (one of the cedars is named after her), learnt to cook in the kitchen and slept in what she described as 'a smallish bedroom top of staircase on right'. As she grew up she acquired a sitting-room of her own with a veranda overlooking the garden.

About a mile away to the north lay East Sheen Lodge, the weekend

Although altered, the interior of White Lodge
retains much of its original decoration and a
fine staircase with a wrought-iron handrail

home of the eldest daughter of the Prince of Wales, Princess Louise, and her husband Lord Fife. Here a few years later a fateful meeting took place. By now Princess May was engaged to marry Queen Victoria's eldest grandson, the Duke of Clarence, but he died of pneumonia in January 1892 shortly before the ceremony. The Princess barely had time to recover from the shock when a substitute was found – his younger brother, the newly created Duke of York, who was to become King George V. Plots were hatched, tête-a-têtes arranged and on 3 May 1893 the reluctant couple, who were hesitant about the Royal Family's speedy matchmaking, were invited to East Sheen Lodge. 'Now, Georgie,' said Louise to her brother after tea was over, 'don't you think you ought to take May into the garden to look at the frogs in the pond?'

Down by the water's edge the Duke proposed and the Princess accepted. They drove to White Lodge, spread the good news and Richmond post office bombarded relatives and friends with telegrams: 'May engaged to Duke of York. Unless announced in papers keep engagement secret.' Queen Victoria had no inhibitions. She ordered the news to be published at once.

Congratulations poured into White Lodge and shortly before the marriage the Tecks organized a huge party. Enthusiastic sightseers jumped up and down trying to see what was happening over the high hedges, deputations presented messages of goodwill and the wedding gifts were dazzling – tiaras, brooches, necklaces studded with diamonds, antique furniture, silver, precious glass and porcelain, carriages, horses, sleighs, boats and a grand piano. As the bride set off for Buckingham Palace escorted by the Household Cavalry, the walls were lined with chests and trunks filled with wedding presents – twenty van loads. In the words of *Lady's Pictorial*, Princess May had become 'the third greatest Royal Lady of Great Britain'.

The following year the Duchess of York, as she now was, returned to White Lodge for the birth of her first child. The Duke, who was the least intellectual of men, sat in the library on the night of 23 June attempting to read *Pilgrim's Progress*. At ten o'clock the baby was born. The child, who was to become Edward VIII and Duke of Windsor, had as his first visitor the Home Secretary and future Prime Minister, Herbert Asquith. A newly installed telephone connected the house to East Sheen post office from where telegrams were dispatched to the Queen and Prince of Wales. Fifteen hundred people arrived the next day to sign a book of congratulations placed in a marquee on the lawn, while flags fluttered in the town and church bells rang out from the rooftops.

Three days later Queen Victoria and her entourage arrived from Windsor. By the afternoon of 26 June large crowds were waiting in the town and on the roads leading to White Lodge. Shortly before half past five a special train bearing the royal party steamed into Richmond

*The Queen Mother's favourite apartment, the
yellow sitting-room, looks out on the garden. Later
she recalled the 'serene peace' of Richmond Park*

Station. Cheers greeted their coming and followed the party along most of the route to the park. Her Majesty stayed an hour and admired the baby – 'a very fine strong Boy, a pretty Child'. Accompanying her was a diffident young man who bore a striking physical resemblance to the Duke of York – the heir to the Imperial Russian throne. Tsarevitch Nicholas had just become engaged to one of the Queen's grand-daughters, Alexandra, and both had come to admire the new baby. Before the end of the year the young couple would ascend the Russian throne and, as the last Tsar and Empress, preside over a tragic reign that led to the 1917 Revolution and their murder.

A month later the Queen, escorted by a detachment of hussars, returned to White Lodge for the christening. Nicholas and Alexandra travelled with her in the royal carriage, but as it was raining the hood was up and the crowds lining the route could see little.

The ceremony took place in the drawing-room in the presence of the Prince and Princess of Wales, the Archbishop of Canterbury, the Prime Minister Lord Rosebery and assorted European royalty. After tea an historic photograph was taken showing four generations. The Queen held the baby on her lap, while the Prince of Wales and Duke of York stood proudly behind her. It was the first time a reigning British monarch had seen three male descendants in direct line of succession.

Richmond organized a day of celebrations while crowds swarmed into the Old Deer Park to enjoy a fête, children's festival, old English sports and swings and roundabouts. The *Richmond and Twickenham Times* described the festivities in a special royal supplement and reported that a Duke of York matchbox containing a 'find the baby' puzzle had a ready sale. The entire cost of the celebrations was only £170–£180 noted the paper with satisfaction – 'It is simply astonishing that such great results were attained at so small an outlay of cash.'

After the excitement of the royal birth a period of quiet descended on White Lodge, but the villa sprang back to prominence in 1923 when the future King George VI and Queen Elizabeth, the Queen Mother, made it their first home when they were Duke and Duchess of York. At the suggestion of Queen Mary, George V loaned them the house and the Queen busied herself decorating the rooms and had a stone staircase built from the drawing-room to the garden. Kitchens and bathrooms were modernized, stables converted into garages and tennis courts improved so the Duke could test his skills against leading players. The Duchess organized garden parties on the smooth lawns and delighted in showing friends round the new home, including her yellow sitting-room with a balcony overlooking the garden.

A few weeks after moving in the royal couple invited the King and Queen to lunch. 'I had better warn you,' wrote the Duke in trepidation, 'that our cook is not very good but she can do plain dishes well, & I know

Children cross a tiny, rippling stream on
stepping stones in the Isabella Plantation – a
woodland garden in the heart of Richmond Park

you like that sort.' Despite forebodings the visit on 28 July passed off amicably, the King was charmed and the Queen thought their home 'very nice'.

Doubts gradually set in, however. The Duke and Duchess had many public engagements and enjoyed dancing and the company of their London friends. Journeying to and from town took a considerable time. During winter the house was lost in fog and on several occasions they had difficulty finding their home as the royal car drove round in circles. In summer sightseers destroyed their privacy, jamming the entrance and crowding round, determined to glimpse the Duke and Duchess. The house was also expensive to run – £11,000 a year. They froze in winter, the electricity proved unsafe and the plumbing unsatisfactory. After three years the Duke and Duchess had had enough. They found a new home at 145 Piccadilly and moved out.

Thirty years elapsed before White Lodge again made news. Shortly after Elizabeth II's coronation in the summer of 1953 the house was surrounded by police. No one was allowed within seventy yards of the building and at night detectives flashed their torches among the encircling trees. Marshal Tito, the Communist President of Yugoslavia, was in residence during a State visit and the government was anxious for his safety. To deter sniper's bullets, folding steel shutters were fixed to his bedroom windows. They are still there, although the room is now a girls' dormitory, for soon afterwards the Royal Ballet School occupied the building. Since then White Lodge has dropped out of history. Members of the royal family, such as Princess Margaret and the Princess of Wales, have paid occasional visits, but otherwise the school goes quietly about its business, isolated and becalmed. 'In winter,' said one member of staff, 'it looks like Bleak House rising out of the mist.'

On the west side of the park lies Pembroke Lodge, originally a mole-catcher's cottage and later home of the Countess of Pembroke. Queen Victoria granted it in 1847 to Lord John Russell, who led the campaign to carry the first Reform Bill of 1832, held numerous cabinet posts and was twice Prime Minister. To his home came the Queen and Prince Albert, Viscount Palmerston who ate enormously 'and seemed to enjoy his food more than talking', Gladstone, Macaulay, Thackeray, Dickens, Browning, Wordsworth, Tennyson, Landseer, Lewis Carroll and John Stuart Mill.

Cabinet meetings were held in the house and a bizarre incident occurred during one of them at the start of the Crimean War. On the evening of Wednesday, 28 June 1854, Earl Russell invited the government, including Mr Gladstone, to dinner. It was hot and sultry as they took their places round the circular table in the dining-room overlooking the glorious view of the Thames Valley. The ministers had assembled at the moment Britain was drifting into war. After the meal

Pembroke Lodge was given in 1847 by Queen Victoria to her prime minister, Lord John Russell, who held many cabinet meetings here

the Duke of Newcastle took out a dispatch and began to read, regaling his colleagues with intricate details of troop movements and the disposition of the fleet. One by one the cabinet fell asleep, Sir William Molesworth tumbling with a clatter from his chair on to the floor. Later, everyone adjourned to another room and the Duke tried again, but the cabinet was too weary to concentrate. The war was a disaster.

More edifying was the visit of the Italian patriot Garibaldi, who called in 1864 to thank Earl Russell personally for helping to secure his country's independence. The Shah of Persia also arrived unexpectedly during a State visit in 1873 when he was caught in a shower of rain. He took shelter in the lodge while the embarrassed Earl apologized for its smallness. 'Yes,' the Shah graciously replied, 'but it contains a great man.'

From 1876–90 the house became the childhood home of the Earl's orphaned grandson, Bertrand Russell, who was brought up by his grandmother and an aunt. The future philosopher, mathematician and social reformer enjoyed careering up and down the steep pathways in his grandfather's bath chair and climbing trees. Especially pleasurable was dropping rotten rosebuds on the roof of the doctor's brougham when he came to the lodge. 'They spread all over with a delicious squish,' he recalled, 'and I withdrew my head quickly enough for the coachman to suppose they had fallen from heaven.'

When he was about seventeen an alarming visitor arrived – Mr Gladstone, with his imperious manner and ferocious stare. After dinner Russell was left alone with the great man and silence descended. Gladstone made only one remark: 'This is very good port they have given me, but why have they given it me in a claret glass?'

Russell was unable to think of a reply. 'Since then I have never again felt the full agony of terror,' he remarked in his autobiography.

Russell's home in Richmond Park had a permanent influence on him. 'I grew accustomed to wide horizons and to an unimpeded view of the sunset,' he said. 'And I have never since been able to live happily without both.'

During the Second World War the lodge became the centre of operations and training for the Phantom reconnaissance regiment, whose members included the film star David Niven. The park was closed for the duration, crops planted, and fifty acres converted into a military camp. The area bristled with anti-aircraft guns.

Occasionally the Supreme Allied Commander, General Eisenhower, whose headquarters were in Bushy Park, came to Richmond to relax. On 24 May 1944, a fortnight before he launched the invasion of Europe, Ike wrote to his wife Mamie describing an evening ride in the park. 'I was all alone … so I could go exactly where I pleased …' At this crucial moment of the war he had a heightened awareness of the surrounding beauty, describing the flowers, trees, rabbits, deer, pheasants, partridges, wild ducks and crows. 'I kept wishing you could be with me to see it … I know you'd have loved it …'

During the war Ike was allocated a suite of rooms in Thatched House Lodge, which was once owned by Sir Robert Walpole. Situated in the south of the park, the lodge later became the home of Princess Alexandra and Sir Angus Ogilvy. Here Princess Anne came in November 1973 with her first husband, Captain Mark Phillips, on their wedding night.

Outside, about 600 red and fallow deer roam through the undergrowth, the less fortunate ending up on royal or archbishops' tables and at Guildhall banquets. In the middle of the park Pen Ponds, created from eighteenth-century gravel pits, teem with wild fowl and fish. Rabbits and squirrels abound.

In the 1950s Superintendent George Thomson created the Isabella Plantation – a woodland garden, laid out with such stagy and romantic artifice that the author Richard Church thought it 'one of the most beautiful retreats which man, in love with nature, has established in this country, indeed in Europe'. Thomson harked back to a pre-Raphaelite vision of beauty: wild flowers, winding footpaths, silvery streams, hidden ponds surrounded by overhanging trees – nature exquisitely tamed. Beyond the enclosing fence lies the park, rambling and wild. This landscape has changed little since Tudor or Stuart times – an extraordinary survival of early rural England. Charles I would recognize some of the oaks that stand today.

Thousands of animals make Richmond Park one
of London's special nature reserves

6 The Golden Years

Embedded in Quinlan Terry's Classical Revival building by Richmond Bridge is a small red-brick house. The bricks are neatly pointed and the façade looks polished and new, but there's something strange – it slopes backwards at a slight angle. Heron House, now refurbished, was constructed in 1693 and is slightly out of true. It was once the home of Nelson's mistress, Lady Emma Hamilton, whom the Admiral called 'My Dear Angel'. Shortly before the Battle of Trafalgar he told her, 'I love you beyond any woman in this world …'

Less than three years after Nelson's death Lady Hamilton came to live in Heron House in the summer of 1808 and stayed the following year. Shunned by respectable society, she was in debt and drank heavily. 'Do not let my enemies trample on me,' she wrote in despair to the Duke of Queensberry. 'For God's sake … dear Duke, good friend, think 'tis Nelson who asks you to befriend, Emma Hamilton.' But her pleas for a pension came to nothing and creditors closed in.

According to her daughter, Horatia, the illness that killed her in 1815 started in Heron House. 'Her illness originally began by being bled whilst labouring under an attack of jaundice whilst she lived at Richmond. From that time she was never well …' Emma drank large quantities of wine and spirits, left Richmond and moved from house to house. After spending ten months in prison she fled abroad and died in Calais shortly before Napoleon was defeated at Waterloo.

During their time together Nelson and Lady Hamilton had the good fortune on one occasion to see the young Edmund Kean acting in *Hamlet*. Kean had prodigious talent, but squandered it in riotous living. By the time he took over the Theatre Royal on Richmond Green in 1831 he was racked by ill-health and alcohol. Although only in his forties, he looked like an old man as he dragged himself across the Green or staggered up Richmond Hill. Work was also killing him and he needed to support himself on the arm of another actor when appearing on stage.

One night his doctor and friend James Smith entered his house, which was next to the theatre, and heard the actor singing. Then the sound died away and there was silence: 'I softly opened the door and went in. His

Lady Hamilton's seventeenth-century Heron House is preserved amid Quinlan Terry's modern 1980s development near Richmond Bridge, but is now an office

head was bowed upon the piano, and as he raised it on hearing my approach a moonbeam fell upon the keys ... they were wet with tears.'

In his last days Kean abandoned himself to weeping and despair. Tormented by thoughts of death, he eventually passed away in 1833 and left behind £600 of debts. The actor was buried in the parish church not far from the Irish peer, Viscount Fitzwilliam, who founded the Fitzwilliam Museum in Cambridge.

During Queen Victoria's reign many great figures of the age came to Richmond. The Queen herself was not only an occasional visitor but also a benefactor. At the beginning of her reign she presented Hampton Court Palace and Kew Gardens to the nation, thus opening them to the public. By then *The Times* newspaper had become the voice of the Establishment. It had been founded by a former coal merchant, John Walter, who is buried in St Mary's parish church, Teddington. At one stage in his career Walter went bankrupt while insuring ships at Lloyds, but soon afterwards he acquired a printing office at Printing House Square in Blackfriars. This, too, proved financially shaky, so in 1785 he supplemented his finances by founding a scandal sheet, *The Daily Universal Register*, which three years later he renamed *The Times*. Walter was a regular worshipper at St Mary's, and when he died on 16 November 1812 he was buried in the churchyard.

About the same time a young boy, who was to become one of the most influential churchmen of the century, was living in a Georgian house at Ham. Subsequently he remembered when he was aged four seeing candles lit in the windows to celebrate the victory at Trafalgar. He lived close to Ham House in Grey Court, Ham Street. The building, which now belongs to a school, bears a blue plaque with the words, 'In this house John Henry Newman (1801–1890), later Cardinal Newman, spent some of his early years.'

Newman loved Grey Court: 'I know more about it than any house I have been in since,' he wrote in later life, 'and could pass an examination in it. It has ever been in my dreams.' To him Grey Court, with its old-fashioned rooms, was 'paradise'. Before he was seven, however, the family moved away and Newman was sent to boarding school.

If the Cardinal was a voice of conscience in nineteenth-century England, so was Charles Dickens, the chronicler of his age. When the novelist came to 4 Ailsa Park Villas in Twickenham in the summer of 1838, he had already published *Pickwick Papers* and was working on *Oliver Twist* and *Nicholas Nickleby*. His wife Catherine was recovering from the birth of their second child and Dickens thought country air would help her recuperate. After writing in the mornings he enjoyed riding, and the couple went boating on the river and visited Hampton Court.

The following year Dickens and his wife moved first to Woodbine

Grey Court, Ham, childhood home of Cardinal Newman. 'I dreamed about it when a school-boy as if it were paradise,' he wrote in later years

Elm Lodge, where Charles Dickens wrote Nicholas Nickleby. 'Beautiful place – meadow for exercise – horse for your riding – boat for your rowing – room for your studying – anything you like,' the author observed

Cottage in Petersham and then to Elm Cottage where much of *Nicholas Nickelby* was written. 'The roads about are jewelled after dusk by glow-worms,' Dickens wrote in the summer of 1839. 'The leaves are all out and the flowers, too ...' Before breakfast he swam in the river from Petersham to Richmond Bridge. 'I myself have risen at 6 and plunged head foremost into the water to the astonishment and admiration of all beholders ...'

Elm Cottage (now Elm Lodge and greatly enlarged) was Dickens' summer home. For twenty years he and his wife returned each year to the Star and Garter Hotel on the summit of Richmond Hill to celebrate their wedding anniversary, and Dickens held a dinner there to celebrate the completion of *David Copperfield*.

What Dickens was to the Victorian novel, Alfred, Lord Tennyson was to poetry. When he arrived in Twickenham in 1851 Tennyson had just published *In Memoriam*, and had become Poet Laureate and married. He rented Chapel House at 15 Montpelier Row, but was soon overtaken by tragedy when his first son was stillborn. Tennyson took a strong dislike to the house and to the district. He also complained about the damp and the smell of cabbages from the nearby market gardens and objected to the 'dirty walks' in the vicinity.

Nonetheless, there were happy moments. His second son, Hallam, was born in Montpelier Row, and among the guests at the christening party were Browning and Thackeray.

Tennyson delighted in the new baby and proudly carried him about the house, showing him to the Irish poet William Allingham, who over the years kept an extensive record of his conversations with the Poet Laureate. 'I could not eat my dinner without a belief in immortality,' Tennyson told him on one occasion. 'If I didn't believe in that, I'd go down immediately and jump off Richmond Bridge.'

Such was his fame that Tennyson was pestered by visitors. Infuriated, he moved to the seclusion of the Isle of Wight in November 1853.

Mary Ann Evans, who broke Victorian conventions by living with her lover, George Henry Lewes, was well aware of the problems fame could bring. 'Whatever may be the success of my stories,' she declared in 1857, 'I shall be resolute in preserving my incognito – having observed that a *nom de plume* secures all the advantages without the disagreeables of reputation.' Thus, when she began publishing fiction, she used the pseudonym George Eliot, a name she adopted when she came to Richmond after living briefly in East Sheen. She and Lewes set up home on the second floor of a Georgian house at 8 Parkshot, near the railway station. A magistrates court now stands on the spot where George Eliot lived for a little over three years from the summer of 1855 until February 1859. Here she created and largely wrote her first novels, *Scenes from Clerical Life* and *Adam Bede*.

*Alfred, Lord Tennyson's home in Montpelier
Row, Twickenham – a fine building in one of
the best early Georgian terraces near London*

Hampton Parish Church, built in 1831 and immortalized by Jerome K. Jerome, lies a few yards upstream from Garrick's temple

The Oxford and Cambridge Boat Race seen from the BBC Radio launch as the crews swing round the great bend at Barnes

George Eliot delighted in the beauty of Richmond. 'We have had a delicious walk in the park,' she wrote on one occasion. 'I think the colouring of the scenery is more beautiful than ever.' The view from the hill had 'a delicate blue mist over it ... As we came home the sun was setting on a fog-bank, and we saw him sink into that purple ocean – the orange and gold passing into green above the fog-bank, the gold and orange reflected in the river ...'

George Eliot found the town less agreeable in summer. 'It is hot, noisy, and haunted with cockneys,' she complained. Twenty years later Henry James voiced similar misgivings about 'crowds of underfed little Londoners' who flocked to Hampton Court and Bushy Park making 'a juvenile uproar under the great horse-chestnuts'. But he admitted nothing could spoil the atmosphere once he was alone and could lie down on the grass in the fading light of evening. He thought the palace 'delightful', but found the paintings disappointing: 'They form indeed a museum of second and third-rate works of art – a kind of pictorial hospital.'

James was in his mid thirties when he came to Richmond. He venerated the famous landmarks and saw the locality at its most lush and sylvan. Food in a riverside inn, however, left much to be desired. Arriving one evening at the 'Anglers' in Teddington, James asked for dinner. 'I am informed that it will be composed of *cold 'am,*' he wrote, exasperated, 'and I can prevail upon my entertainers to add nothing else to the *menu.*'

One afternoon James displayed an unexpected athleticism by rowing 2½ miles from Richmond to Teddington and then walking along the tow-path to Hampton Court. He also went to Barnes Bridge early one morning to watch the Oxford and Cambridge boat race. Standing among 'a dingy British mob, with coal smoke ground into its pores', he glimpsed the two crews as they shot Barnes Bridge – 'great white water-swimming birds, with eight feathered wings'. The result was unique – the only dead heat in boat race history.

The match was first rowed over the 4¼ mile course between Putney and Mortlake in 1845. During Victorian times and up until the 1960s the banks and bridges were crowded with thousands of people who swarmed to see the annual race, but television has depleted the racegoers and many now prefer to watch the event at home. Nonetheless, rowing flourishes, canoeists paddle contentedly over the placid waters and families and day-trippers go afloat in summer. At Hampton, Constables, established in 1867, still make and hire out beautifully crafted skiffs – wooden boats about twenty-four feet long – that once graced the river in Victorian times. At night, a canvas tent converts the craft into a tent with room for three people on board.

Such a craft was used by Jerome K. Jerome's *Three Men in a Boat.* The men actually existed – Jerome himself, George Wingrave (a bank manager) and a photographer, Carl Hentschel, who was the model for Harris. Only the dog, Montmorency, was invented. Jerome maintained his book was based on a trip they made up river in 1889, although he coloured the incidents.

One of the places where Harris insisted the three men stop was Hampton church, which is about 200 yards upstream from Garrick's villa. The present church, whose foundation stone was laid by the Duke of Clarence, was constructed in 1831 and built on the site of an earlier building whose graveyard was haunted by bodysnatchers. Harris's interest in history was limited. He wanted to laugh at Mrs Thomas's monument – 'She's a lady that's got a funny tomb, and I want to see it.' Curious visitors have trooped to the church ever since, expecting something bizarre. Instead they find a charming eighteenth-century sculpture. 'A noble composition,' declared Pevsner, 'though the figures of the semi-reclining mother and seated daughter are not very sensitive.'

The river, of course, provided inspiration for writers and painters. Thomas Rowlandson produced a graceful collection of local views. As a boy, J.M.W. Turner lived for about a year in Brentford and from 1805 frequently sketched and painted on the river. The first watercolour that John Ruskin acquired from the artist was a view of Richmond Hill and the Bridge. As the most influential critic of the day, Ruskin was an eloquent champion and declared the painting 'had nearly everything *characteristic* of Turner in it', with tossing trees, picnickers frolicking on the embankment and the delicate arches of the bridge and misty outlines of the hill enveloped in a golden haze of sunlight.

On many occasions Turner would go afloat with large canvases, or wooden panels, and paint directly from nature. But the artist also drew inspiration from his favourite poet, James Thomson, whose lines he sometimes attached to his paintings, notably *Richmond Hill, on the Prince Regent's Birthday* (1819), one of his largest works. Thomson's vision of landscape – with shifting light and movement and 'the magic art of colours melting into colours' – foreshadowed the theories of Impressionism and Turner's own diaphanous images.

Turner was so attracted by Richmond and the surrounding countryside that in 1807 he bought a plot of land at Twickenham for £400 so he could build himself a house near Sir Joshua Reynolds' home on the hill. The small Italian villa, called Sandycombe Lodge, was designed by the painter and was his occasional home from 1813–26. Here, a few hundred yards from Marble Hill and Orleans House, he lived with his father in such simplicity that according to a friend, 'The tablecloth barely covered the table ...' The house contained model ships, which are recognizable in his paintings, while fir trees close to the lodge adorned his classical landscapes, as did nearby river views and the countryside.

*Britain's greatest artist, J.M.W. Turner, designed
and built Sandycombe Lodge at Twickenham and
from 1813–26 lived within the landscape he painted*

Cattle graze in Petersham Meadows, a reminder of how London's riverside once looked. The land is preserved by Act of Parliament. Van Gogh got lost here one night in 1876

Petersham Church, with Georgian box pews. The Queen Mother's parents married here. Outside in the churchyard lies the explorer Captain Vancouver, who circumnavigated the globe

Turner enjoyed fishing in the Thames and dug a square pond in his garden where he could deposit his catch. Sometimes the garden was invaded by local boys who raided blackbirds' nests which Turner tried to protect – earning himself the nickname of 'Blackbirdy' from the youngsters.

In 1815 he was invited to Orleans House to meet the exiled French King, Louis-Philippe. Many years later, when the painter visited France, the King presented him with a gold snuff-box encrusted with diamonds.

Turner has been called 'the Father of Impressionism' and two members of that school were at work in Richmond upon Thames later in the century – Sisley and Pissarro. In the summer of 1874 Alfred Sisley stayed at Hampton Court, and within a few weeks produced sixteen paintings. Sisley captured a sunlit Thames with scudding clouds and boating on sparkling waters – old Hampton Court Bridge; Molesey regatta with flying crews hunched over their oars, billowing flags and waving spectators; Molesey lock; the weir with swimmers about to plunge into the river; Barge Walk. This was 'The perfect moment of impressionism', claimed the art critic Kenneth Clark. 'I doubt if a picture could be much truer to a visual impression, with all its implications of light and tone, than the Sisley paintings of Hampton Court.'

Down river at the corner of Gloucester Road and Kew Green a blue plaque commemorates Camille Pissarro's visit in 1892. He lived in a flat above a bakery and painted a number of oils of Kew Gardens, the Green and St Anne's church.

Van Gogh, on the other hand, produced no paintings during his stay in 1876. He was twenty-three, tried his hand at schoolmastering and preaching, but had yet to find his vocation. While living in Holme Court, Twickenham Road, Isleworth, he became a Methodist preacher and worshipped in a small wooden chapel in Petersham and Richmond Methodist Chapel.

Van Gogh arrived a year before Henry James and, like the author, visited Hampton Court. He, however, appreciated the paintings in the palace, enthusiastically itemizing works he thought 'very beautiful' and 'splendid'. He delighted in the countryside and in lyrical letters to his family described the local landscape and ambles along the Thames beneath the trees. One November evening, however, he got lost while trying to cross Petersham Meadows. 'At last I saw a light in a little house,' he wrote, 'and climbed and waded through mud to reach it.'

Regrettably, Van Gogh produced only a couple of sketches of some local buildings and Petersham chapel. That chapel has since disappeared, but a significant event happened nearby in the still-existing St Peter's church on 23 July 1881 – the marriage of Lord Glamis and Miss Cavendish Bentinck. The *Richmond and Twickenham Times* filled two columns, listing 160 guests and their wedding presents and informing its

Trumpeters at the Royal Military School of Music,
Kneller Hall, where 130 army bandsmen are trained
each year, many from the Commonwealth

readers that the inhabitants ran strings of flags across the roadway. Later, during the reception in the bride's home at Forbes House on Ham Common, 'In accordance with an old family custom, Lord Glamis and his bride sat at the head of the table under a large bell composed of roses, and when the bride cut the cake the bell was swung.'

Nine years later the couple welcomed the birth of a daughter who was to marry George VI and become Queen Elizabeth the Queen Mother. 'When I was very young I often used to visit my grandmother at Forbes House,' she later recalled. 'It had then a lovely garden and a home farm with a herd of Jersey cows.'

Four months after the marriage of Lord and Lady Glamis the local paper carried a story that sent shivers round royal circles: GRAND DRAMATIC PERFORMANCE, trumpeted the headlines, A BRILLIANT SUCCESS. In November 1881, the most notorious woman in Britain, Lillie Langtry, the Prince of Wales' mistress, appeared on stage for the first time in what the paper called 'a truly dainty piece of acting'. Mrs Langtry was as intelligent as she was beautiful, but at twenty-eight she realized the Prince's attentions were wavering. So were hers. That March she had secretly given birth to an illegitimate daughter fathered by Prince Louis of Battenberg (Lord Mountbatten's father). In order to support herself and her daughter, she decided to pursue a career as an actress.

Her first appearance was at a charity performance of *A Fair Encounter* in Twickenham town hall, organized by the dramatic actress Mrs Henry Labouchère. The hall was crowded with fashionable society, including Oscar Wilde and the first man to swim the English Channel, Captain Webb. Lillie played Lady Clare St John. 'The appearance of Mrs Langtry in an elegant costume,' enthused the local paper, 'was greeted with prolonged applause … her acting was exceedingly creditable …' Other papers recognized her talent and Lillie went on to pursue a successful career after the royal ardour had cooled, appearing not only in the West End but also at the new theatre on Richmond's Little Green. Opened in 1899, the theatre was designed by Frank Matcham, who was responsible for the Coliseum and London Palladium. Richmond's theatre would attract some of the greatest names in entertainment – Charlie Chaplin, Ellen Terry, Donald Wolfit, Ralph Richardson, Alec Guinness and John Gielgud.

The theatre catered for increasing numbers of people who came to live in the borough in Victorian times. The opening of Hampton Court and Kew Gardens encouraged visitors and the river attracted day trippers who came by train. Constructed in the middle of the nineteenth century, the railways opened up Richmond to tourists and made it and the surrounding villages easily accessible from London. Professional people could now work in town and live in the suburbs. Soon vast numbers of buildings sprang up – houses, shops, schools, factories, hospitals and

*One of the strangest sights on the river –
a chalet brought from Switzerland in
1882 and erected on the embankment near
Tagg's Island*

*Boys fish opposite Tagg's Island
where Edwardian houseboats
hug the bank and the impresario
Fred Karno built his financially
disastrous fun palace.*

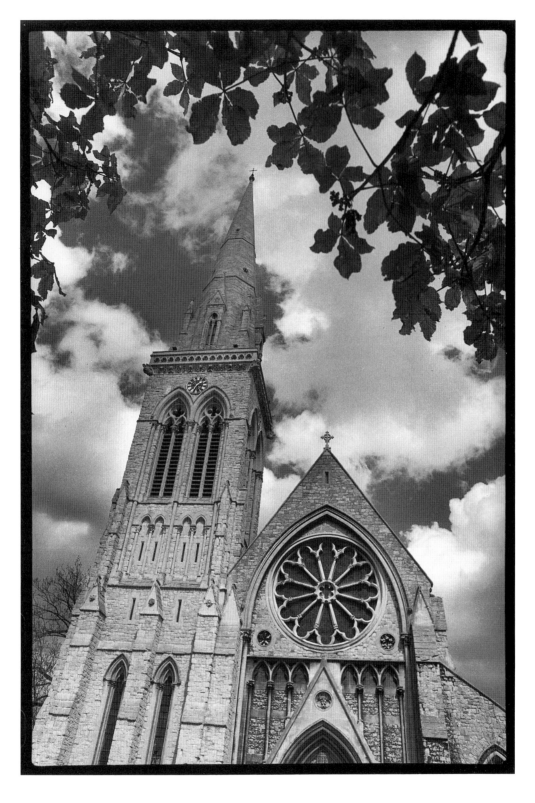

St Matthias' Church, Richmond Hill, designed by Sir George Gilbert Scott. The controversial Victorian architect planned hundreds of buildings, and had his drawing office in a gardener's cottage in Ham

The body of the Victorian explorer Sir Richard Burton is housed in this extraordinary tomb in Mortlake – 'An Eastern tent standing amid alien palms in a little corner of English earth besides the Thames'

almshouses – until the villages were linked one to another, with an occasional architectural surprise. Opposite Tagg's Island near Hampton Court, a local land owner put up a genuine Swiss chalet in 1882. He used it as an annex to his riverside home. The chalet had a boat house at ground level, a billiard room on the first floor and a gaming room above. It is now part of Hucks' Boatyard.

Kneller Hall in Whitton became the home of the Royal Military School of Music. It was established in 1857 by the head of the army, the Duke of Cambridge, following a musical disaster at a grand ceremony to celebrate the end of the Crimean War. The army massed together a number of regimental bands, but none could play at the same tempo or in the same key. Even the National Anthem proved beyond them. In modern times, the army's principal school of music has trained about 130 bandsmen each year, and its trumpeters are frequently heard on State occasions.

New churches also featured prominently, the most visible being Sir George Gilbert Scott's St Matthias, perched on the summit of Richmond Hill with a spire nearly 200 feet high. Scott was the most prolific nineteenth-century architect and designed the Foreign Office, the St Pancras Station Hotel and that spiky symbol of the Victorian age, the Albert Memorial. The cost of his Richmond church was just over £10,000.

In Mortlake, Catholics built St Mary Magdalen. The graveyard contains the tomb of the explorer Sir Richard Burton. As a boy he had lived for a year in Richmond (his family occupied a house in Maids of Honour Row) and gone to the Revd. Charles Delafosse's school on the Little Green, where he was involved in constant fights with other pupils. Burton pioneered exploration in central Africa, discovered Lake Tanganyika with John Speke in 1858, and was a writer of distinction and translator of *The Arabian Nights*. He also translated Oriental sex manuals, such as *The Perfumed Garden*, which his horrified wife Isabel discovered and burnt after his death, along with his Rabelaisian diaries and journals.

Burton objected to being buried in the earth or cremated. 'I should like us both to lie in a tent side by side,' he told his wife. When he died in 1890 Isabel built one of the strangest mausoleums in London – an Arab tent twelve feet square and eighteen feet high – constructed from rippling stone and marble to resemble canvas.

Isabel was a staunch Catholic and Burton's friends were outraged when her agnostic husband was given a religious funeral. Many boycotted the ceremony. Inside the tomb mourners found an altar and Arab lamps. 'I have sent to the desert for strings of camel bells,' said Isabel, 'which will hang across the tent, and like an Aeolian harp when the wind blows, the twinkle of camel-bells may still sound near him.'

Isabel took a cottage at 2 North Worple Way and each Sunday visited the mausoleum and held seances there. Today the curious can see inside the tomb by climbing an iron ladder at the back and peering through a glass window on the sloping roof. Below lies the death chamber – a grey, dusty room, with a broken crucifix and red and white flasks strewn upon the altar, while from the ceiling dangles a cracked oil lamp. Plaster peels from walls hung with religious images. Burton's coffin, made from sheet steel and ornamented with gilded lions and angels, lies to the right opposite Isabel's plain mahogany coffin.

'He has got the very thing he wanted,' said his wife, 'only of stone and marble instead of canvas – to be buried in a tent above ground; to have sun and light and air, trees, birds and flowers …'

Sir Richard Burton's dust-covered coffin. The marble mausoleum was badly damaged by vandals seeking non-existent treasures, but restored in the 1970s and is now a listed building

7 Garden City

In 1889 a vast new church was built in Teddington – St Albans, in Ferry Road. Its flying buttresses and green copper roof soaring above the trees are visible from Richmond Hill. It resembles a cathedral, or rather half of one, for the money ran out and it was never completed. John Betjeman described St Albans as 'a fine, soaring Gothic Revival building … it looks like a bit of Westminster Abbey that has been left behind upstream'.

This religious curio is noted for its associations with the actor and playwright Noel Coward. 'I was baptised into the Church of England,' he declared, 'and, I believe, behaved admirably at the font. No undignified gurglings and screamings.'

He did on one occasion, however, dance down the aisle. The church was the centre of Teddington's social life. The Coward family, who were 'fiercely musical', took an active part in the services and his father and mother first met during choir practice and married in St Albans. Until 1905 the family lived at 131 Waldegrave Road in a pleasant semi-detached house backing on to the railway line.

In August of the following year Charlie Chaplin, who was only in his teens, appeared in *Casey's Circus* at the Richmond Theatre; he returned three years later to star with Stan Laurel in *Humming Birds*. Chaplin was working for the music hall impresario Fred Karno and visited him on his luxurious houseboat, the *Astoria*, at Tagg's Island. The floating home – ninety feet long and costing £20,000 – resembled a miniature liner with mahogany panelling and marble-lined bathrooms.

Just before the First World War, Karno built a fun palace on Tagg's Island – a new hotel, ballroom, stage and ice-rink set in ornamental gardens. An electric ferry linked the island to the shore and there were a hundred boats in which the guests could enjoy themselves on the river. Known as the 'Karsino', the fun palace cost £70,000. Initially concert parties, military bands, fireworks and dance bands attracted the wealthy, including Lord Curzon, Lady Diana Cooper and C.B. Cochran. But Tagg's Island was too out of the way, people failed to come, and the war and bad weather destroyed it. By the mid 1920s Karno was bankrupt and his folly was demolished in the 1970s. After immense struggles with the

Teddington Lock, the upper tidal limit of the Thames. The largest lock – 650 feet long – can take a tug and six barges

local council the island was converted into a haven for houseboats with a lagoon, though a few steps that led down to the river in Karno's time are still visible. The *Astoria*, meanwhile, was beautifully preserved. Eventually she was moored upstream near Garrick's Temple and occupied by the lead singer and guitarist of Pink Floyd, David Gilmour.

Karno's disaster contrasted with the success of the Royal Richmond Horse Show in the Old Deer Park, which started in 1892. George V and Queen Mary came three years in succession, including 1913 when the show attracted the King and Queen of Portugal, Queen Alexandra and the Dowager Empress of Russia. The Duke and Duchess of York were guests when they moved into White Lodge after their marriage in 1923, and Queen Elizabeth II attended in 1952 and 1958. The show was held annually for seventy-five years, but closed in 1967 due to rising costs and falling income. It has since been revived.

International rugby matches were also played in the Old Deer Park until Twickenham became the game's home. In 1906 the Rugby Football Union wanted a permanent headquarters for the England team. They found a market garden near Kneller Hall, which frequently transported soldier musicians to and from London by train. The London and South Western Railway agreed to build two extra platforms to take special trains on international match days, thus making a rugby ground feasible. The first game was played at Twickenham in 1909 between Harlequins and Richmond. The world's first live sporting commentary was broadcast from the ground on 15 January 1927 when Captain H.B.T. Wakelam described a match between England and Wales for BBC Radio. Propped up in front of his microphone was a card with the admonition, 'Don't Swear!'

Today the headquarters is housed in modern brutalist buildings (concrete with high tech flourishes) seating 75,000 people. These dwarf the Rowland Hill Memorial Gate on top of which stands a golden lion. Made from artificial stone in 1837, the lion stood for many years in front of a brewery on London's South Bank. When that building was replaced by the Royal Festival Hall in 1951, George VI insisted that the lion be saved. Eventually it was acquired by Twickenham rugby ground, hoisted into a place of honour and covered with £6,000 worth of gold leaf – a gleaming symbol of the British Lions.

Meanwhile, in 1904, the composer Gustav Holst moved to Grena Road, Richmond, where his daughter, Imogen was born. In 1907 the family moved to 10 Barnes Terrace. The composer's new home was a bow-fronted eighteenth-century building by the river, near the railway bridge. 'He had a large music room on the top floor,' remembered his daughter, 'and in the evenings the grey, muddy river would collect all the colours of the sky and shine with a magical light that filled his three windows.' The house also provided a good view of the Boat Race and

Fred Karno's luxurious houseboat, Astoria, *whose marble and mahogany interior resembles an Edwardian liner, is moored on the river at Hampton*

A flood wall protects composer Gustav Holst's home from the river at Barnes

Virginia and Leonard Woolf set up the Hogarth Press in Paradise Road, Richmond

A family of geese savour the plants near Barnes Pond

The Golden Lion of the Rugby Football Union

Holst invited his friend Ralph Vaughan Williams to see the crews racing by.

The nearness of the river, however, had drawbacks. At high tide water overflowed the embankment and seeped in through the front door and the damp atmosphere affected the composer's health. Nonetheless, during his stay at Barnes he composed the opera *Savitri*, *A Somerset Rhapsody* and *Beni Mora*. When he left Barnes in 1913 he started work on the suite that brought him international fame – *The Planets*.

The following year Virginia Woolf and her husband Leonard came to live in Richmond. Virginia was recovering from a nervous breakdown, having twice been confined to a nursing home in Twickenham. Her attacks coincided with overwork, and Leonard thought Richmond would provide a quieter life than London. The couple spent the first few months at 17, The Green, but later moved to Hogarth House in Paradise Road, their home for nine years. Here Virginia suffered another breakdown. She claimed she heard 'the voices of the dead' and lay in bed 'mad, and seeing the sunlight quivering like gold water ...' When violent, she needed four nurses to restrain her.

After nine months, Virginia recovered. Thinking manual work might be therapeutic, the couple bought a small hand-press and in 1917 started a publishing company, the Hogarth Press, in their dining-room. Here they produced about forty books, including Katherine Mansfield's *Prelude*, Maxim Gorky's *Reminiscences of Leo Tolstoy* and the first edition of T.S. Eliot's *The Waste Land*. The Hogarth Press also published works by John Middleton Murry and E.M. Forster and Virginia's own short story, *Kew Gardens*. The house was filled with luminaries – Clive Bell, Maynard Keynes, Lytton Strachey, Vita Sackville-West and Lady Ottoline Morrell.

Virginia appreciated the beauties of Richmond Park and Kew Gardens (the Pagoda was visible from the back windows of Hogarth House) and found strolling by the river agreeable, though on one occasion she was cut off by flooding and had to 'creep along a railing so as to reach dry land'. Although Virginia thought Hogarth House 'beautiful and lovable', she found Richmond too remote and in 1925 she and Leonard moved back to central London.

The previous year George V and Queen Mary had opened the Royal Star and Garter Home for Disabled Sailors, Soldiers and Airman, built at the top of Richmond Hill on the site of the hotel that had been destroyed by fire. Down below, the Royal British Legion set up their Poppy Factory in Watney's Brewery and used Cardigan House as a social club, until it was replaced by flats. Disabled workers have been employed in the factory since 1926 and donations for the forty million Armistice Day poppies they make each year help ex-Servicemen and women.

As the population of Richmond and the surrounding villages grew in the inter-war years, there was a demand for more places of worship.

Making some of the 40 million Armistic Day
poppies that are produced each year at the Royal
British Legion Factory

Money was limited so ingenious solutions were needed to provide new churches. Are not barns 'the Cathedrals of Agriculture' it was asked? The owners of a splendid specimen with soaring pillars and vaulted roof at Hurst Green, in Surrey, thought so. Soon this Tudor building was dismantled beam by beam and transported to North Sheen where it was re-erected as a church. Marks made by cattle rubbing their horns against the wood are still visible. The Bishop of Southwark consecrated the barn church in 1929 in the presence of 800 people.

Equally strange was the fate of Wren's All Hallows church, Lombard Street, in the City of London. Dubbed 'the invisible church' because it was surrounded by City buildings, All Hallows' future was threatened when the foundations shifted and the walls cracked. At the outbreak of the Second World War the 104-foot-high white stone tower was dismantled and re-erected in Chertsey Road in Twickenham, eleven miles away from where the architect had built it 250 years before. A modern and much larger church was constructed alongside. This contains fittings from the original Wren building, including monuments, the reredos, organ, royal coat of arms and carvings. All Hallows also contains the pulpit in which John Wesley preached his first extempore sermon in December 1788. Wesley forgot his notes and was 'under much mental confusion and agitation', but his improvisation proved so successful that he never again wrote out a sermon.

About the same time that All Hallows appeared in Twickenham, a future prime minister and his new wife moved into a modest two-room flat nearby. Harold Wilson was a statistician in the civil service and learning about the inner workings of government. Mary disliked Twickenham and they moved to another flat, 19 Fitzwilliam House, on the Little Green close to Richmond Theatre. Harold became a Labour MP in 1945 and shortly afterwards the youngest cabinet minister since Pitt. Their son Robin was born in Richmond and the family kept the flat until 1948 when they moved to Hampstead Garden Suburb.

Richmond was the Wilsons' wartime home, and during both world wars local factories produced aircraft, and local boatyards constructed wooden motor torpedo and coastal craft. Notable among the boatyards was Thornycrofts on Platt's Eyot, opposite Hampton Waterworks. Although the firm has long since departed, the island retains its First World War atmosphere with many of the original buildings intact, including the huge wooden doors on one of the boat-building sheds.

Downstream at Teddington Wharf, Tough Brothers, who began building boats in the 1820s, constructed fast naval vessels and fire boats, many of which tackled the fires in the London docks during nightly raids by enemy aircraft. In May 1940 Douglas Tough and his staff were caught up in Operation Dynamo, the evacuation of Dunkirk. Britain's newly appointed Prime Minister, Winston Churchill, ordered small boats to

The Wren church that moved – the tower of All Hallows, Chertsey Road, once stood 11 miles away in the City of London

rescue allied soldiers trapped by the German army on the French coast. In a few days Tough collected about a hundred craft from their moorings, stripped out the loose gear, filled them with fuel, found suitable crews and sent them down river.

Altogether the boats the Tough Brothers assembled rescued 5,000 men. Douglas Tough's forty-foot motor yacht, the *Thamesa*, took part in the evacuation. Later it featured in television films, and at the height of the Beatles' popularity in the 1960s it smuggled the musicians up the Thames to Teddington Studios to avoid the crowds.

During the war, from 1940–5, Richmond and Twickenham suffered 1,217 air raid alerts; 241 people were killed, hundreds injured, nearly 800 buildings destroyed and over 43,000 damaged. Everyone had to endure rationing and the blackout. In Teddington all the ducks disappeared. Local people ate them.

Hidden away amongst trees at Ham Common lay the most sinister secret of the war – Latchmere House. The counter-intelligence agency MI5 converted this Victorian mansion into a clandestine interrogation centre – Camp 020 – in July 1940. Nazi spies were brought here for questioning after parachuting into the country, or landing on remote beaches. Soon the building was ringed by barbed wire, a high double fence and armed guards. Interrogators eavesdropped on prisoners in their cells by means of microphones hidden in the ceilings.

The camp's purpose was to turn round spies and persuade them to work for the allies as double-agents, feeding false information to the enemy, an audacious plan known as Doublecross. Agents who refused to co-operate were either hanged or shot. Since spies were excluded from the Geneva Convention, Camp 020 operated outside the law and was never inspected by the International Red Cross. Officially it didn't exist. This enabled the commandant, Colonel R.W.G. Stephens (known as 'Tin-Eye' because he wore a monocle), to subject prisoners to brutal pressure. Many were humiliated and threatened (dummy executions were organized at night); some attempted suicide and one was almost beaten to death.

Few local residents knew what went on inside the camp, and forty years passed before the truth was revealed. Latchmere House is now a rehabilitation centre for ordinary prisoners. One of the Great Train Robbers was an inmate and peacocks stroll through the grounds.

Covert operations also took place in Teddington, where the aeronautical engineer and inventor, Sir Barnes Wallis, tested models of his bouncing bombs that skimmed along the water and destroyed the Ruhr dams in Germany. Experiments were conducted at the National Physical Laboratory in Bushy Park. Sir Barnes mounted a catapult at the end of No. 2 tank and fired spinning balls up the tank: 'One of the officials, who didn't believe there was anything in my claims, was

Period boatyard buildings at Port Hampton, Platt's Eyot

The borough's guiltiest wartime secret – Camp 020, Ham Common

For six generations Tough Brothers have built boats. Robert Tough in his Teddington boatyard with Dunkirk veteran motor yacht, Thamesa standing just behind me. When he saw this ball go skipping up the tank I heard him say, "Oh my God!" ' The experiments proved successful and in May 1943 the Dam Busters – 617 Squadron – attacked and destroyed the Mohne and Eder dams.

A few hundred yards from the laboratory, concealed beneath camouflage nets, lay Camp Griffiss, headquarters of the US Eighth Army Air Force and the US Strategic Air Force in Europe. It was here that thousand bomber raids on German cities were organized, including the Dresden attack that killed 35,000 people. In charge was America's foremost air commander, General Carl Spaatz, the highest-ranking wielder of strategic air power. Camp Griffis, code-named Widewing, was situated in a corner of the park between Chestnut Avenue and Sandy Lane. Later in the war the Supreme Allied Commander, General Dwight D. Eisenhower, moved his headquarters here so he could gather together allied planning staff and mastermind Operation Overlord – the invasion of Europe.

Eisenhower arrived on 5 March 1944 to find a cluster of Nissen huts, tents, an airstrip and nearly 3,000 men barricaded from the adjoining village by a brick wall ten feet high. Supreme Headquarters Allied Expeditionary Force (SHAEF) occupied long, low buildings – damp, unheated and with cement floors. Eisenhower's office, in Building C, was simple and unpretentious with two telephones, a dark brown carpet, ordinary chairs and sofas, three flags and a tidy desk for Ike believed in efficiency. Work began at 8 a.m. and often went on for twenty hours a day.

To Bushy Park came nearly every important allied figure in the Second World War, including Churchill and the Cabinet, the Chief of the Imperial General Staff Field Marshal Alanbrooke, Montgomery of Alamein and Generals Bradley, Patton and Alexander, as well as Air Chief Marshals Harris, Portal, Leigh-Mallory and Tedder (Ike's deputy). There were so many generals at SHAEF that they had their own mess from which other officers were excluded. George Patton, the foul-mouthed, erratic but brilliant commander, dined wearing ivory-handled pistols despite a rule forbidding firearms in the mess. Forever embroiled in controversy, he was summoned to Bushy Park on 1 May after provoking uproar with an ill-considered speech. Ike intended sacking him, but there followed one of the most bizarre incidents in the war. Patton, who was highly emotional, apologized, burst into tears and rested his head on Ike's shoulder, whereupon his helmet clattered on to the floor. Eisenhower thought the scene 'ridiculous' and abruptly ended the interview. Patton kept his job – just.

Decisions taken in Bushy Park decided the fate of western Europe and its shape after the war, but there were lighter moments. Joe Louis put on a boxing display. Film stars Clark Gable and James Stewart, who served

The greatest invasion in history – D-Day – was
organized on this spot in Bushy Park where General
Eisenhower set up Supreme Allied Headquarters

in the forces, entertained the troops. So did comedians Bob Hope and Ben Lyon. And on Sunday afternoons the band leader Glenn Miller serenaded the officers and men and made one of his last appearances here before vanishing during a flight over the English Channel.

On 6 June Eisenhower launched the greatest invasion in history. As the allied armies sped across Europe he returned thirty times to Bushy Park to confer during the next two months. On 10 June his boss, General George C. Marshall (author of the postwar European recovery plan), arrived with his team, accompanied by Churchill. Ike gave them a cheerful tour of his headquarters, showing them where his forces were on the maps, and later took them across the Channel to the beaches. Marshall was impressed, telling President Roosevelt that Eisenhower and his staff were 'cool and confident' and carrying out a complicated task with 'superlative efficiency'. As Ike put it, 'The smell of victory was in the air.'

Bushy Park played a vital role in winning the Second World War and the Americans were popular with people in Teddington. Local residents were shocked therefore when the camp was demolished in 1962. Despite protests every building was torn down and the site grassed over. No memorial mentioned the invasion headquarters, let alone the general who liberated Europe, created NATO to protect it and afterwards became President of the United States. Only the name of a small road outside the park, SHAEF Way, indicated something extraordinary had happened.

It was not until the fiftieth anniversary of the Normandy landings in 1994 that action was taken. Excavations revealed that a foot below the surface of the ground lay the foundations of Eisenhower's office. Parts of his pot-bellied heating stove were also dug up. The floor, which was 20 feet square, was reinstated and a plaque unveiled to mark the site. A new pedestrian gate – the SHAEF Gate – was installed at the former camp entrance in Sandy Lane.

At the end of the war an elderly mariner, who had rescued 130 troops from Dunkirk, moved to east Twickenham and set up a boatyard at 1 Ducks Walk, opposite the site of the old Tudor palace. Richmond Slipways, as it was called, mostly repaired police boats – a sedate life for Commander Charles Lightoller, a man whose career was crammed with adventure. He had gone to sea when he was 13, survived four shipwrecks, been marooned on a desert island, mined gold in the Klondike, rammed and sunk a German U-boat with his destroyer in the First World War and been active in the Second. He was also the only senior officer to survive the *Titanic*'s disastrous maiden voyage in 1912 and miraculously escaped drowning after being sucked down under water as the liner sank. The Commander passed away peacefully in his Twickenham boatyard just before Christmas 1952.

Lightoller was very much a figure of his time – loyal, patriotic and

The site of General Eisenhower's SHAEF office, Bushy Park

Titanic hero Commander Lightoller's boatyard in Twickenham

Craftsmen at George Sims Racing Boats, Eel Pie Island, make traditional wooden craft for clubs, universities and international oarsmen

conservative – but the world was moving on. In the liberated 1960s Richmond was caught up in the social and cultural revolution that swept the country. The crime of the decade, The Great Train Robbery, was planned in Twickenham. There, in a flat at 214 St Margaret's Road, the gangster Buster Edwards helped organize what was then the largest ever mail hold-up – £2.6 million. The austere, yellow-brick Victorian house was only yards from Ailsa Avenue, where the Beatles shot the opening scenes of *Help!* And the avenue was close to Twickenham Film Studios where other 1960s classics were produced – *Saturday Night and Sunday Morning, Accident, Alfie* and *The Italian Job*.

The first ever newspaper report about the Rolling Stones appeared on 13 April 1963 in the *Richmond and Twickenham Times*. The group was performing at the Station Hotel, Kew Road. 'The deep earthy sound produced at the hotel on Sunday evening,' wrote Barry May, 'is typical of the best of rhythm and blues that gives all who hear it an irresistible urge to "stand up and move".' The Stones, whose average age was twenty, had attracted only fifty people when they first appeared at the hotel, but within weeks attendances rocketed to 500 and the doors had to be locked on screaming fans. Even the Beatles came to hear the new sound, and by August there was hardly room to dance. Mick Jagger was quoted as saying, 'It gets so crowded that all the fans can do is stand and twitch.'

Young people who had temporarily deserted Eel Pie Island in Twickenham, where jazz bands had played since the 1950s, returned in droves when the new stars – the Stones, The Who and Elton John – performed there. During the tumult hippies moved in and the authorities refused to renew the licence of the island hotel, which eventually burnt down. Eel Pie Island, which originally housed boatyards and shacks and had a nautical flavour, reverted to normal. Many residents still live in quaint Emett-like bungalows, while hammering and banging come from marine engineers repairing a cabin cruiser or Thames launch. George Sims, the only makers of wooden racing boats on the tideway, have their works here. They built eights for both crews in the 1971 Oxford and Cambridge Boat Race.

In recent years the island's charms have been eroded by insensitive development and modern houses have gone up on the site of the hotel. More generally, much damage has been done to the borough by tactless planning. When, in 1952, the Queen Mother reopened Richmond's Old Town Hall which had been badly damaged in the war, she warned of the danger of destroying 'unostentatious and gracious houses' in Richmond and Ham. Her grandmother's home, Forbes House, had been pulled down in the 1930s and she noted another was about to disappear. 'Progress I know cannot be halted by sentiment,' she said, 'but let us, at least, be sure that it is progress before we destroy, and that we are not losing more than we are gaining.'

*Intellectual nourishment – a sec-
ondhand bookshop at Hampton*

*Richmond College, the American Inter-
national University on Richmond Hill*

*Rugby at St Paul's School, which has over 750 pupils and is one of the
oldest public schools in England*

Unfortunately, the Queen Mother's warning was ignored. From the mid 1950s until the 1970s Britain embarked on a vast rebuilding programme from which no one could escape. Although an attempt to tear down and rebuild the centre of Richmond was resisted, in the 1950s the eastern side of Richmond Park was ruined by the towers of Roehampton's Alton Estate, where Le Corbusier's baleful architectural vision became a reality. When St Paul's School moved to a forty-acre site in Barnes near Hammersmith Bridge in 1968, another opportunity to design buildings in harmony with their surroundings was lost. The school, founded in 1509 by the Dean of St Paul's, John Colet, numbered amongst its pupils Milton, Pepys, Marlborough, Judge Jeffreys and Field Marshal Montgomery. The new premises resembled office blocks and factory buildings.

A hundred years before Henry James wondered whether Richmond was too beautiful. It had reached 'a climax of maturity', he averred. It was 'over-tame ... like a country that is over-ripe; that cannot afford any more mellowing'. Soon, there was a reaction. In 1901 developers tried to demolish Marble Hill and build houses on the site, a project that would have ruined the view from Richmond Hill. Public indignation provoked an Act of Parliament to preserve that part of Richmond's riverscape, but in the following decades developers got their way elsewhere. In Twickenham aggressive high-rise offices rose near the station and Cardigan House was torn down on Richmond Hill and replaced by ugly flats. The whole borough was tarnished with clumsily designed homes, offices and shops. Richmond Green was disfigured and graceless houses erected a hundred yards from Richmond Bridge.

The government appeared to declare architectural war on the borough when it dumped the Public Record Office on the embankment at Kew, close to where Turner and Pissarro had produced their delicate paintings and Decimus Burton his Palm House. In a wilful defiance of beauty, the nation's memory was housed in a gigantic concrete building resembling a bomb shelter. Millions of Britain's records, from William the Conqueror's Domesday survey to present-day government papers, were hoarded in a building of uncompromising brutality.

It was left to Post-Modernists to reassert traditional values and produce architecture on a human scale. The way forward, they claimed, was to look backwards. The developers of the most sensitive site in the borough by Richmond Bridge called in the Classical Revivalist Quinlan Terry. 'The traditional methods of the Georgian and Victorian builders remain the best,' asserted Mr Terry. 'Architects started to go wrong when we departed from these time-honoured principles.' Instead of concrete he dared to use bricks – 5,000,000 of them – and a whole dictionary of architectural styles, including Venetian Gothic. This splendid pastiche was damned by Modernists. 'I dislike it intensely,' scoffed the President

Quinlan Terry's spectacular challenge to modern
architecture in the 1980s – conserving the best and
invoking the past by Richmond's historic bridge

of the Royal Institute of British Architects, Maxwell Hutchinson. He thought the offices 'sickly' and the whole development stagy and self-indulgent. But many local people approved. In *Building* magazine Martin Spring applauded the 'superb fanfare of classically turned rooftop cupolas and turrets which pick up the romantic skyline of trees and buildings cascading down Richmond Hill'.

Terry retained existing structures, such as the Italianate Tower House, Lady Hamilton's Heron House and the Old Town Hall. The largest modern building was modelled on William Chamber's ideas for a new palace at Richmond and a Palladian gateway leading from Heron Square to the river was adapted from the Basilica at Vicenza. Behind the façades and grouped round three squares lay offices, flats and shops. Hidden underground were two car parks, while a landscaped terrace swept down to the Thames.

Elizabeth II showed her approval by officially opening the development on 28 October 1988, and the Prince of Wales praised it. 'You will not find the fool's gold of the "International Style", which has spread over so much of our world, represented here,' he declared with satisfaction.

Terry produced the most important architectural statement in Richmond in the twentieth century. And Post-Modernists have built more sensitive buildings in the borough, notably in Twickenham near York House and the parish church. Earlier, in 1972, American educators saved a handsome Victorian building, the disused Wesleyan Theological Institution, by converting it into an international university – Richmond College. Built on top of Richmond Hill in 1843 in neo-Tudor style, the main façade resembles an austere version of Wolsey's Hampton Court, but finished in white stone rather than brick. The college occupies five acres of grounds, shaded by trees, and attracts students from more than eighty countries.

A few hundred yards down the hill George III's workhouse at Pesthouse Common fell on happier times. The tramp cells had been closed in the 1920s and the building became an old peoples' home. Then, in the 1980s, the former workhouse was converted into luxurious flats.

Nineteenth and twentieth-century developments transformed the borough's isolated towns and villages into a garden city. The film-maker Richard Lester, who made Petersham his home in the 1960s, was enthusiastic about the blend of town and country:

> Our land is filled with badgers and foxes; there's a heron next door; we have owls falling into the house – any number of marvellous birds – woodpeckers. It's a rural life, very quiet … This is suburbia at its best, the link between pure countryside and the ability to go up to the West End and see a show in half

Teddington Weir Suspension Bridge – Victorian and as essential to the fabric of the working river as grand houses, villas and vistas

an hour … From an architectural and sociological point of view there's nothing to beat it.

Nonetheless, admirers need a selective eye. Too often ugliness obtrudes. Along the river boatyards, which gave so much life and character to the area, were replaced by houses and flats lacking all nautical feeling and clashing with the historic landscape. In the 1990s heritage groups intervened. The Royal Fine Art Commission, the Countryside Commission and English Heritage invited the landscape architect and environmental planner, Kim Wilkie, to devise a plan to protect 'one of the most remarkable metropolitan landscapes in the world' – the eleven miles of the Thames between Kew and Hampton.

Writing in his *Tour through the Whole Island of Great Britain* in the 1720s Daniel Defoe had praised 'the distant glory' of the buildings along this stretch of river. He was the earliest person to realize that the total setting with its views and avenues of trees was more important than isolated villas, palaces, gardens and parks. Now, over 250 years later, Wilkie devised a plan that considered the area as a whole. He wanted to open up the lost seventeenth- and eighteenth-century landscapes that inspired painters and writers and clear away scrub and undergrowth on the riverbank masking landmarks. Interwoven with the royal and aristocratic landscape was a working river with ancient waterfronts, boatyards, wharves, period houses, boatclubs, islands, pubs and walks that were vital to the atmosphere and needed preservation, or sensitive updating and redevelopment. 'Obviously we can't order the immediate demolition of past mistakes – buildings which block historic views, and so on,' declared Mr Wilkie. 'But there may be a point in the future when they can be rectified.'

So, as Richmond upon Thames moved towards the twenty-first century local people were determined not only to guard existing beauty, but use it as an inspiration for what was to come. The setting in which they lived had more than domestic importance; it was linked with national identity. Damage here injured Britain's heritage. A once private and privileged landscape for royalty and the Court was open to all, but constant vigilance was needed to prevent destruction. In future, whenever a new building was contemplated, three questions needed asking: Is it elegant? Is it good mannered? And does it fit in? The answers would determine the fate of the borough.

The White Swan, Twickenham. This riverside
inn, once called the Swan, has been a centre of
social life since the early eighteenth century.
Balconies were added a hundred years later